THE NEAR EAST

AND THE

GREAT POWERS

THE NEAR EAST

AND THE

GREAT POWERS

WITH AN INTRODUCTION BY RALPH BUNCHE

EDITED BY RICHARD N. FRYE

KENNIKAT PRESS, INC./PORT WASHINGTON, N. Y.

THE NEAR EAST AND THE GREAT POWERS

Copyright 1951 by The President and Fellows
of Harvard College
Reissued 1969 by Kennikat Press by arrangement

Library of Congress Catalog Card No: 77-79309
SBN 8046-0530-0
Manufactured in the United States of America

~~~ Preface ~~~

It should be unnecessary to justify a publication on the contemporary Near East at the present time.* Though the Far East has usurped the headlines of late, all nations in Asia are vitally important as members of the free world. This is especially true of the countries of the Near East, rich in oil and strategically located. Many are the problems, internal as well as international, which beset the peoples of this region of the earth, and in the year 1951 their problems have become our problems. It is incumbent upon Americans, with our world-wide responsibilities, to better understand the peoples of the Near East. This we can do only with knowledge, sympathy, and—as Charles Malik says—with love. But it is a two-way proposition; the peoples of the Near East must also understand us. H. A. R. Gibb points out the need for *mutual* understanding, *mutual* respect, and a concept of *mutual* service, if we are to succeed in our relations with the Near East.

The core of the Near East is the Arab world and Israel, and we have concentrated on that core in this book. Authorities on the Near East, from the academic profession, from government, and from business, have contributed to make this publication more representative of current thinking about the area. Many problems have been left untouched, for their number is legion, but we have felt that a combination of general discussions with papers on special topics would provide a better understanding of the area as a whole. Thus topics range from the broad, philosophical discussion of Charles Malik to the detailed account of the struggle for unity in Syria and Iraq by Majid Khadduri.

* In American usage, the designations "Near East" and "Middle East" are synonymous, with the latter more popular since World War II. I have preferred the former since we are not concerned with Iran or Turkey in this book, and since it also avoids confusion for non-American readers.

PREFACE

The substance of the book was first presented in the form of papers and remarks by participants in a conference entitled *The Great Powers and the Near East,* held at Harvard University on the afternoons and evenings of August 7, 8, and 9 of 1950 as part of the Summer School program of conferences. It was originally conceived by Professor William Y. Elliott, Director of the Harvard Summer School, as a supplement to the program of courses on the contemporary Near East.

The proceedings of the conference were recorded on tape, but it was decided that the papers would not be published as they were delivered. Rather the material would be rearranged and presented in a more logical order. In this way kindred topics would be grouped together and greater unity would be achieved in the publication. Several papers were enlarged after the conference, so what is here presented is more than what was heard by the audiences during the six sessions of the conference.

The program of the conference—with the order of papers and remarks on them as delivered—is given in Appendix II.

The views expressed in the various papers are those of the several contributors and do not represent the opinion or preferential selectivity of the editor. I have not changed the colloquial flavor of some of the papers.

I wish to thank again all of the participants in the conference and the staff of the Summer School. Without their aid and cooperation the Summer School courses, the conference, and this publication would have been impossible.

RICHARD N. FRYE

≈≈≈ Contents ≈≈≈≈≈≈≈≈≈≈≈≈≈≈≈≈≈≈≈≈≈≈≈≈≈≈≈≈

vii

CONTENTS

II · THE NEAR EAST

THE PALESTINE PROBLEM

THE ARAB WORLD

INTRODUCTION

THE NEAR EAST AND THE GREAT POWERS

RALPH BUNCHE

Introduction

Several points in regard to the Near East would seem to merit special consideration and concern by Americans. First, I think it vital to bear in mind that despite the success of the United Nations in putting a stop to the war in Palestine, the Near East remains a troubled area, and from the standpoint of the pattern of peace, it is still a danger spot. With regard to the aims and policies of the great powers, it is not very clear what their ultimate objectives in their Near Eastern policies are, and I have in mind particularly the United States and the United Kingdom. If doubts exist as to the aims of the policies of these nations, it may certainly be doubted that their policies in the Near East are reaping, or for that matter are likely to reap in a time of crisis, any handsome dividends. For example, what might we expect from that area in the event of a showdown between East and West? What is the situation now? I think it must be clear that neither the United States nor the United Kingdom commands any great popularity in the Near East. In the course of my work there I found it was no advantage whatsoever—quite the contrary—to be an American, until the period was reached when resentment against the British, for their failure to support the Arabs in the Palestine conflict, took some of the heat off the Americans. Then I at least had the advantage of being able to say I was an American and not British.

The attitude of the Near Eastern states to the greatest crisis con-

1

fronting the United Nations—the Korean crisis—and the urgent appeal made for effective assistance in support of the United Nations efforts in Korea, is especially significant. The Arab world, as is well known, is sorely divided, at least politically. Its military potential even for defensive purposes is probably not very great. The present peace between the Arab states and Israel, which is based solely on the armistice agreements, is insecure despite the provisions in those agreements against aggressive acts by either party, and doubtless it will remain insecure until the outstanding differences, especially that concerning Arab refugees, have been solved.

In the Arab world, as I found it, there is resentment at the position of the United States on Palestine, and general suspicion of our interests in the area—particularly our oil interest—and these feelings are only less severe with regard to United Kingdom policy. I recall that Arab leaders often told Count Bernadotte and myself, in the course of our negotiations, that while they were opposed to the creation of a Jewish state in Palestine, on the obvious grounds of what they considered to be gross injustice against the Palestine Arabs, their opposition in a more fundamental sense was based on the fear that the establishment of a Jewish state would create in the Near East a new bridgehead for imperialist intrusion. When we would ask them what kind, who would be on this bridgehead, they would say, "It may be Americans; it may be Russians; it doesn't matter too much." They argued always that they had suffered greatly from such intrusion in the past. They never failed to bring up this argument as the most fundamental one in explaining their position with regard to the Palestine question.

What does the United States, what do the democracies really seek in the Near East? Are we seeking to find there or to establish there another bastion of democracy, Western style? Certainly the Near East is not that today and I do not know who would be prepared to prophesy that it is likely to become so in the reasonably near future. Democracy, in our sense, is no strong force in that region, and so far as I can see there are no encouraging indications that it is likely to become such a force. Are we primarily concerned with strategic bases, having in mind the Suez Canal, oil interests, and geography? It is always well to bear in mind that past experiences have demonstrated amply that such bases are of dubious value if they are in the midst of a hostile or even indifferent population. Nothing that I know of would be any more reassuring to the West in this regard than the unhappy experience in the last World War.

Then there is the real problem, the basic problem—thinking always in terms of American interests and the American approach —which is to be found in the realm of our relations with peoples and our attitudes toward them. With regard to our ability or perhaps inability to make an impact which nurtures understanding, which inspires mutual confidence and sympathy, the plain fact is, I think, that the United States—and probably the United Kingdom and the Western democracies generally could be included—has not shown an ability to establish a firm and sympathetic rapport with people such as those found in the Near East, in the Far East, and in Africa—a oneness and a sense of fellow feeling which will tend over a period of years to align these people with us. It may be that Americans, whether they are tourists or officials or businessmen, have not excelled in the task of winning friends and influencing people in a lasting way. This is especially true in areas such as the Near and the Far East, areas in which there are to be found important differences in race, religion, and culture, and where there is poverty, widespread misery, economic underdevelopment, and social distress. Confronted with such challenges, we Americans, too characteristically perhaps, tend to think largely in terms of dollars as a panacea. But often we do not invest those dollars wisely or well in terms of our future relations with the peoples concerned. Thus, most fundamentally, we need to come to a realization that it is not necessary for people to do things as we do them, to live and think like us, to order their social and economic and political lives on an American model or something approaching it, in order for them to be good people, people worthy of our full respect and understanding.

Perhaps there is a certain unintentional, unconscious, cultural egotism, certainly not deliberate, something which may derive from what at times appears to be an excessive self-righteousness on our part, to be found in our approach to other peoples. We are usually too materialistic and we are frequently paternalistic toward them, though in a very friendly and most cordial way. When American G. I.'s in the last war in North Africa and the Near East referred to Arabs as "Ayrabs," this was something a little more than just a mispronunciation. It was something of the same color as the employment of "gooks" in the Pacific, a term which unfortunately, according to dispatches, may have cost us some good will in Southern Korea today.

I think of an experience not so long ago in the United Nations. One of the finest, most broad-minded, and most sincere of American representatives became involved in a heated debate on the Palestine question, and around the table were seated representatives of Israel and the Arab states. In his emotion and his determined resolution to make his point in the best American tradition, he suddenly pointed his finger at the Arab and Jewish representatives and told them, "What you people need to do out there is to be good Christians." He did not say "good American Christians." That was probably a slip of the tongue.

I feel that we need something much more than the dollar sign as our impact on the peoples with whom we come in contact. It may be that there is a certain element of cultural lag in the relations of the United States and the United Kingdom with the peoples of the Near East. The British and other Western powers have had a background—the colonial approach, the colonial attitude, a sort of special approach to backward peoples, an unfortunate survival perhaps of the romanticism of Kipling's days—which was a tendency to think a little too much in terms of the "white man's burden." One finds reactions and often strong reactions to this sort of approach, or to what is interpreted as being this sort of approach, on the part of people with whom one comes in contact in such areas as the Near East and the Far East. It is not enough for us to say finally as we say, and say with utmost sincerity, that we as Americans stand squarely for freedom, for the sanctity of human rights, for the dignity of man. We must find an effective way, and I do not think we have begun to find it yet, of translating these ideals into reality for millions, scores of millions, even hundreds of millions, of peoples in far-flung areas who have as yet not even come to have an understanding of the concepts themselves. That will take a tremendous effort and perhaps a good deal of money, but more than that, and taking first things first, it will require a most farsighted and statesmanlike policy and program: a policy and program which may in the nature of the case often cut across the political policies of expediency and of immediacy which are all too apparent in times such as these. Indeed, it might well, in areas such as the Near East, find us involved in revolutionary changes of very great magnitude in societies. But we must weigh what the alternative may be in terms of the present conflict in the world, in terms of the techniques employed by those who would set up an order on a quite different basis from the one to which we adhere.

It seems self-evident that our policy should always be such as to find us squarely on the side of the people. If we are to discharge our present immensely heavy and unparalleled responsibilities effectively and with dignity, we have first of all a vast job of self-education to undertake. Cultural understanding is something which properly must begin at home. We need to realign our human relations' sights in the most basic way, in order that we may come to think of peoples in the Near East, the Far East, the Caribbean, and Africa—with regard to their abilities and potentialities—as equals, really as equals, and to be able to treat them as such in our policies and actions in a convincing way. That, I think, is one of the most imperative jobs that we in this country have to do in meeting the new responsibilities which have come to us as a result of the role of leadership assumed by this country since the end of the last war.

I. THE GREAT POWERS

POLITICAL AND ECONOMIC FACTORS

H. A. R. GIBB

Introductory

The subject of the relations of the Great Powers with the Near East is neither an easy one nor is it a comfortable one for any of us. We have to realize that the Near East is not just last year's problem, over and done with, but that it remains a major, current problem, and that each one of us who lives in a democratic country is, in a sense, individually responsible for it. It may be fortunate, for this reason, that it falls to a Britisher to open this series of papers, because none of the powers concerned in the events in the Near East since the end of the last war has come out of it with clean hands and untarnished honor. All of us have been guilty of sins and shortcomings, and before we go on to discuss the sins and shortcomings of others we must first humbly confess our own, and recognize how far our actions have contributed to the conflicts and confusions into which the Near East has been plunged.

There is no way by which the policies of any of the governments involved can be morally justified. I am not going to speak here, at this moment, about the failures of Arabs or Zionists, but about ourselves. At the root of the errors of our western democratic governments lies the ignorance of the people about the Near East, and, because of this ignorance, their susceptibility to one-sided propaganda. It was because of this that the British governments of the interwar years, against the advice of the Foreign Office, adopted that shilly-shallying, temporizing, and incoherent policy which ultimately not only lost for Britain the substantial object of British policy in the Near East—I mean the creation of an integrated and friendly bloc in the whole area—but also deprived her of reputation and honor. The same factors have underlain the policy and action of the United States. It is not for me here, or anywhere, to criticize the policies of the American government. But there is one fact so essential to an understanding of the present situation, not only in the Near East but in Asia as a whole, that it must be firmly and openly stated. The methods by which the Near Eastern policy of the United States was forced through the Assembly of the United Nations in 1947 not only undermined at one stroke, through much of Europe and all of Asia, the authority of the United Nations, but also undermined respect for the integrity of the United States in its dealings with the United Nations.

That is why the problems of the Near East, and an adequate and accurate knowledge about them, are more vital for the United States than most Americans realize. For the consequences of our actions remain with us. The Near East is not only on our hands but on our hearts. Your country and my country are deeply entangled in it, whether we like it or not. We cannot pull out of it; we cannot just leave it to its own peoples. There is no way out of the tangle until all parties, American, British, Arabs, Zionists, learn to look at the situation and at their own part in producing this situation squarely and honestly, and to face the realities behind their hopes and fears, their aspirations, jealousies, beliefs, and cynicisms.

CHARLES MALIK

The Near East Between East and West

You are all excited today about the Far East; how do you know tomorrow you may not be even more excited about the Near East? Perhaps the deferred excitement may prove even more exciting. The Far East is "between" East and West in a somewhat accidental and transient sense; the Near East is fundamentally, essentially, permanently "between" East and West.

There are a number of preliminary distinctions and definitions that one would ordinarily feel bound to make at the outset of a paper like the present one. I shall dispense with these preliminary matters. I shall only assume three things: that it is obvious that because of the enormous diversities in the Near East, the propositions I shall entertain apply only differentially to its various parts; that the reader is fully capable of discerning by himself this discriminating application without my having to belabor this point at the start; and that he is fully aware of the political, economic, and above all strategic importance of the Near East.

II

The Near East is neither East nor West, nor a synthesis of East and West.

It belongs to a separate, more grounded inquiry to show that this negative characterization of the Near East is perhaps its most distinctive characterization. The Near East is certainly something in itself, but even this "something in itself" can be shown to be more a negative function of something else—that is, *not* something else—than an ultimate self-referring and self-explaining thing.

The Near East is not the East, notwithstanding the obvious presence of traces of Hindu mysticism in the Near Eastern spirit.

For there are radical differences between the basic and dominant Near Eastern character, on the one hand, and either the Chinese character, founded on the whole upon social, ethical, and family relationships, or the Indian metaphysical-Hindu outlook, which in its typical instance tends to consider everything worldly, historical, or material, a mere shadow, on the other hand.

Nor is the Near East the West, notwithstanding the indisputable historical influence of the Near East upon the essence of the Western tradition, and the well-known impact of the West upon the Near East in medieval as well as modern times. That the Near East, despite all this historical interaction, is not the West is due to two acts which occurred, one in the Near East and one in the West, and which now determine the being of the Near East and its relations to the West.

The Near Eastern act was of course the establishment and entrenchment of Islam. Although Islam has a high regard for Christ, although the Virgin Mary is revered by Islam, and although there are obvious Hebrew-Christian influences in the Koran and especially in certain phases of Sufism, yet Islam cannot be said to have bodily taken over and adopted the Christian heritage. Islam was more a substitution for, than a development and a completion of, an existing system. Thus Islam came to be quite distinct from Western Christian spirituality. Nor was Greek thought, despite its fine interpretation by the great Moslem-Arab and Christian-Arab philosophers, ever deeply absorbed into the thinking and literature and general outlook of Arab or Moslem culture, so as to make this culture an authentic heir of that thought in the same way in which European culture has certainly authentically inherited it. This, then, is the first act, originating in the Near East, which amounted at least to a partial rejection of the West.

But there is a second act, originating this time in the West, which amounted to a rejection of the Near East by the West. Ever since the days of the Crusades the West has neither felt nor made the Near East feel that the Near East is part of the West, that there is a peaceful, normal interaction between the Near East and the West, that the Near East is the brother, or at least the cousin or partner, of the West. Though all the ultimate values which the

West holds sacred, and by which it is characterized, owe their origin to the Near East, the Near East has invariably been made by the West to feel as though it were a stranger, an outsider, if not an enemy. Whether this Western rejection of the Near East is a reaction to the original Moslem rejection of the West, or whether this latter rejection was itself but a negative response to an earlier thoughtless and unloving rejection of the Near East by the West in pre-Moslem times, is an interesting question, certainly worthy of an entire detached investigation. But this question is quite irrelevant to our present purposes; for whatever the causes, the fact remains that there has been and there is today a marked reciprocity of estrangement and rejection between the West and the Near East.

Furthermore, the Near East is not a synthesis of East and West, notwithstanding the simultaneous existence, in a seething, eclectic fashion, of traces and tinges of both the Eastern and the Western spirits in the bosom of the Near East. A genuine, original, abiding, responsible synthesis of East and West, one that understands, absorbs, reconciles, rises above both East and West, has never been accomplished; at least it has never been accomplished in the Near East—though the Near East, due mainly to its middle geographical position, is perhaps the natural place to expect such a spiritual synthesis to occur. It is true there are some today who seem to expect such a synthesis from the Indian world. But genuine cultural syntheses are no easy matters. If there is anything unutterable in history, it is precisely such syntheses. Nor do they occur by simply juxtaposing diverse cultures; when they occur, they are the creative acts of terrific crises and cataclysms. Those who seek or talk in terms of so-called syntheses seem to me always to be impatient with the immediately given: they are in a hurry to overcome it without sufficient regard to the true and eternal. What if certain things do not mix! What if it is better to have them apart for a long time, or at least for a while!

Though all these negative determinations, in themselves, merely define what the Near East is not, they nevertheless point to the existence of a Near Eastern character *sui generis;* for, though the Near East is not something else, or a synthesis of other things, it is certainly *not nothing.* The intrinsic character of the Near East is

13

not and never has been closed, isolated, a function merely of itself. The Near East arose and developed as an active agent struggling with both the East and the West, partly rejecting, yet partly accepting and assimilating some of what it knew of the East and the West, in the manner in which it understood them. It was through this active confrontation, at once negative and positive, that it came to its own. This distinctive being of the Near East is of course Islam, with its history and traditions and institutions and civilizational structures.

In a fundamental philosophy of culture, the Near East can be shown to exemplify the category of "the between." Perhaps it is *the* instance of this exemplification. It is neither East nor West, nor quite a combination of them, nor even a connecting link "between" them; it just "lies between" them. I assure you the precise determination of this character of "betweenness" with respect to the concrete being of the Near East is a fascinating topic for responsible research.

III

I have so far referred to "East" and "West" in their traditional, more authentic and therefore proper acceptation. We must also inquire into the position of the Near East vis-à-vis the ideological situation of the present day. It is a false usage to employ the terms "East" and "West" with regard to the present ideological conflict. In the first place, communism would have been impossible without classical German idealism and the social and economic phenomena of early nineteenth-century British industrialism. Thus communism is a Western phenomenon, however one must finally determine its precise relation to the true spirit of the West. In the second place, I believe there is no trace of the genuine spirit of the East in Marxism-Leninism-Stalinism. In the third place, India—to take a most outstanding example—lies outside the communist orbit; and although it must always be remembered that India itself refuses to be placed elsewhere than in itself, yet, in so far as one *must* place it somewhere, it is more correct to place India at least alongside the non-communist world. I shall therefore refer not to a conflict between East and West, but to a confrontation between the communist and the non-communist worlds, where the effective agent in the one case is Soviet Russia and the effective agent in the other case is, if not the United States, then certainly the Atlantic Community. Referring briefly to this Community as the West, one may speak of a conflict between Soviet Russia and the West.

Where then does the Near East stand in this conflict?

This is an important question. It cannot be adequately treated in the compass and with the presuppositions of this paper. If, however, we have regard to the truth, and to the truth alone, then I believe the following topics will have to be investigated in a thorough examination of this question.

(1) A distinction must be made between the attitude of governments and the attitude of peoples, in so far as peoples are in a position to form an attitude.

(2) A distinction must be made between sheer political interest and the presence or absence of a spiritual affinity with the West or with communism: namely, between relations of expediency and relations based on a community of ideas.

(3) It is commonly held that there is something in the Near East that is basically foreign to communism. From this assumption certain political cynics have concluded that the West can do almost anything it pleases with the Near East without fearing that it would turn in the direction of communism. As one such cynic put it once, "No matter how deep a wound we may inflict on this or that part of the Near East, and no matter how much then it might look upon us as enemies, still it would remain faithful to us, because from its point of view communism is far worse." "In this instance,"—I am still quoting the cynic—"the maxim: the enemy of my enemy is my friend, does not apply. Therefore we can be quite bold in our dealings with the Near East." Of course the cynical politicians are wholly incapable of fathoming the truth; therefore the world, under their enlightened guidance, moves from one mess to another. But in order really to determine the truth or falsehood of this belief, the following points must first be ascertained in all responsibility and truth:

A. Whether the religious sentiment is sufficiently strong to withstand a socio-economic onslaught of the communist type.

B. Whether communism is not resourceful enough to make use of the religious sentiment itself.

C. Whether the unrelieved, though perhaps unconscious, misery of the masses—economically, socially, and politically—could not be awakened into conscious articulation by the communist message; especially so long as the socio-economic meaning of the West has been highly ambiguous.

D. Whether the supra-nationalism of the Soviet Union, namely, the overcoming of narrow nationalism by vigorous attachment to an imperial center and by political inclusion within a vigorous imperial idea, whether this supra-nationalism does not appeal to a region which has known imperial existence far more than nationalistic fragmentation.

E. Whether communist universalism by comparison with Western particularism, especially in regard to race and culture, does not strike a responsive chord in the heart of a region whose highest creations have always been forms of spiritual and human universalism.

F. In respect to the basic categories of existence, namely, the human person, truth, reason, spirit, nature, matter, force, history, love, forgiveness, the higher things, freedom of the individual, the collective, the sense of security, the sense of belonging, the possibility of difference and rebellion and nonconformity, the totalitarian idea, the Byzantine identification of temporal and spiritual power: in respect to these categories, all talk about the real relation between the Near East on the one hand, and communism and the West on the other, is pathetically superficial until the theoretical and actual place of these ultimate categories in the life and being of the Near East, the West, and communism is fully and responsibly determined.

I believe a carefully executed program of research based on this outline will reveal three things: (1) that the Near East is not basically opposed to communism; (2) that the West is under illusion if it supposes that there are no limits to the liberties it can take with certain parts of the Near East because there is no danger it would, of itself, ever turn communistic; and (3) that despite everything it is perfectly possible to win the confidence of the entire Near East if the West in certain respects undergoes a real and abiding change of heart.

IV

I propose to dwell if but for a moment on the political situation; for in the Near East the political these days is prior to the social and economic. It even overshadows the religious and ideological. Certain sections of the Near East seem to be satisfied politically with respect to the West; this certainly cannot be said of the Arab world.

Political grievances, generated by the policies of the Western powers towards the Arab world, outweigh in the popular mind any ideological affinities or antipathies that may exist between the Near East and the West or between the Near East and communism. In a situation like this, anti-communist propaganda sounds extremely abstract and hollow, especially in view of the fact that communism has a more vigorous and dynamic appeal to the popular imagination than any half-hearted and unconvincing presentation of the case for democracy.

The long list of pledges voluntarily given and arbitrarily withdrawn, of divisions dug deep in the social structure and hostilities encouraged among groups and countries, of dark regimes established and upheld, of open alliances resulting in the creation of permanent threats to the Arab countries, of lost opportunities when badly needed help and guidance were simply withheld; it is these things which, casting dark shadows on the minds of the people, will not fail to arouse deep anxieties for generations to come.

The political record of the Western powers, so far as the Arabic-speaking world is concerned, has not been very happy. Putting aside the few political friends of the West whose friendship is based on obvious reasons, the genuine friends of the West include some of our intellectuals who are inspired by the truer image of the authentic West. They do not fail to see the difference between their conception of the West, formulated through their acquaintance with the deepest spiritual achievements of the Western spirit, and the more immediate image of the materialistic, utilitarian, intriguing, and exploiting West of politico-economic commercialism. *These*

17

friends of the West—and in view of the difficult situation under which their friendship is put to the test, they really merit the title of "friends"—are not blind to the dichotomy in the soul of the West today: the discrepancy between the deepest that the West was and is and stands for, and the tangible reality of the West as it acts and unfolds the symptoms of its present crisis. If they maintain their faith and their hope and their love; if they hold in check their understandable inclinations to doubt; if they—not without inner crises of the spirit—put aside for the time being the political grievances which they share with their countrymen—if they do all this, it is not because they feel the plight of their countries less, or care less sincerely for the destiny of their peoples. They do so because they believe that the flame of truth and justice and love at the heart of the West has not been and can never be extinguished, that the West they know and love has not died and can never die, that the real Christian spirit of the West—whereby the West means, or ought to mean, only to be helpful—will not fail, in God's time, to reassert itself, and that one day the West, when it awakens to itself, to its dangers and to its possibilities, will surely redress the injustice it has visited upon the Near East. But, in the nature of the case, such believing, loving, unwavering, undismayed friends are not many. To the overwhelming majority the gross political realities are completely disillusioning.

V

Let us now turn to the future. Being is the future falling back upon the past in order to utilize the present in the fulfillment of its transcendent ends. What can be done to promote a better understanding, a happier and more fruitful association, between the Near East as a whole and the West?

Let me state first that such fundamental tasks do not yield either to hysteria or to magic or to miracle. They are the benign fruit only of profound understanding and care. If there is sufficient care, a way out will always be found. But the care must be both sufficient and genuine. Although I shall presently state my views on this all-important question, let me first assure you that any nervous expectation of a magical formula that will swiftly and easily produce

18

results will be disappointed. There is no short cut to creative confidence; only hard work, patience, vision, guilelessness, and a firm self-grounding on the truth will, in the end, avail.

(1) For the last one hundred and fifty years the Near East has been, so far as its relations with the outside world are concerned, in constant and almost exclusive contact with Western Europe and America: politically, economically, culturally. This in itself is a valuable foundation. Accordingly, what is required is not a creation *ex nihilo,* not an indiscriminate break with the past, but a qualitative transformation of attitude and policy whereby the West can justly utilize and wisely build upon this priceless heritage of interaction, despite all its unhappy aspects and episodes. A judicious sense of continuity is sobering under the present circumstances. But such a sense of continuity presupposes that the West realize and act on the realization that in the end it is the one hundred million Moslems and Arabs of the Near East who are going to determine its destiny, and not extraneous forces.

(2) There are valuable democratic elements in the Near East. By "democratic elements" I do not mean anything fantastic or absurd; I mean people who have arisen from the masses, who therefore know and feel with their situation, who have a genuine sense of social responsibility, who despise darkness and place a premium on freedom, who crave for economic and social justice, who hate autocracy, who are responsibly conversant with the great issues that shake the world today, and who are in genuine communion with the Western positive tradition. If these elements are lovingly and courageously sought and supported, they are likely eventually to help in undoing the present alienation between the Near East and the West. It is the foremost task of those who are genuinely concerned for the destiny of the Near East to unearth the positive elements of light and truth, to draw them out of their dormancy and shy retreat, into the sunshine and fresh air of struggle and responsibility, and to encourage and help them to come to their own.

(3) The West should have a genuine interest in the peaceful, free, independent development of political institutions in the Near East, and a conscious policy for the promotion of conditions of

political stability in that region. So long as certain situations remain chronically unstable, how can the best elements plan and accept responsibility for the long pull? Now the region between direct, crude interference and complete unconcern is pregnant with unexplored possibilities; and the seizing of opportunities within this intermediate region is an accomplished art, the creative work of concern itself.

(4) The movement of contact between the Near East and the West in recent decades has been characterized by conspicuous disunity in Western policy. This is the inner significance of the celebrated "Eastern Question." Thus, for instance, the Arab world is an arena of strife and jealousy among the Great Powers. Competition for the oil of the Arab world is a major phenomenon in the world situation. Unless the Western Powers harmonize on the highest level and on a long-term basis their policies with respect to the Near East, and unless in this harmonization the Near East is treated not as a means only but as an end to be respected in its own right, it is hopeless to expect stability or peaceful development in that most sensitive part of the world.

(5) The joint Declaration issued by the Governments of France, the United Kingdom, and the United States on May 25, 1950 seems to me to be a step in the right direction. However, it could have been made less ambiguous; that is why a great deal depends on the mode and spirit of its application. Despite all this, the response of the Arab League to it has been positive and statesmanlike, thus giving fresh evidence of the desire of the Arab world to encourage and build upon any hopeful sign of improvement in Arab-Western relations.

(6) The Arab mind must be thoroughly disabused of the obsession that in certain fundamental conflicts of interest some Western Powers will in the nature of the case always side against the Arabs. While this obsession lasts, there can be no peace and no confidence. Surely then a specific declaration in this regard is indicated, whereby the highest authorities assure the Arabs—and the assurance is periodically made good—that their interests will not be cyclically encroached upon.

(7) There is another thing that is obviously indicated. Three im-

portant resolutions of the United Nations with respect to the Palestine problem have not as yet been implemented, and there are no indications that any effort is being made towards their implementation. I refer, of course, to the resolutions regarding the frontiers, the internationalization of Jerusalem, and the fate of the one million Arab refugees. I do not believe that a wholehearted United States' support of these measures will fail to contribute effectively towards their realization. If the United States does this, it will only be respecting the will of the international community, expressed in each case by more than a two-thirds majority of the United Nations. People cannot understand why decisions by the United Nations affecting the Far East are sacred while those affecting the Near East are not as sacred. I believe that nothing can restore the confidence of the Arab world in the West as much as a bold and honest support by the Western powers of the standing resolutions of the United Nations.

(8) A bold policy must be devised for arming the Near East and enabling it to participate effectively and responsibly in its self-defense. For questions of security should be a coöperative affair. It is bad politically and morally both for the West and for the Near East if the Near East feels that it is being "protected" militarily. There is a vast reservoir of manpower which could certainly be trained to play its part in the service of world peace. In fact there is nothing to have prevented this force from being in existence today except a certain myopic vision which has afflicted certain quarters for thirty years.

(9) There are certain outstanding questions which Egypt rightly feels should be settled. A diplomacy that aims at promoting positive understanding between the Near East and the West ought to be resourceful enough to satisfy Egypt in this regard. Constructive proposals to this end can certainly be made.

(10) Consider, further, the Turkish demand for inclusion in the Atlantic Treaty. The point of this demand is that Turkey feels— and I believe rightly—that if the Near East is important for the defense of the West, some juridical linkage ought to be established between its system of defense and that of the Atlantic Community. Existing assurances in this field are important, but the exigencies

of the moment make it quite plain that these assurances are not enough.

(11) A statesmanlike application of Point Four on a large scale in the Near East is imperative. But the flow of private capital and the extension of technical assistance are not enough. In addition, public financial assistance is requisite for all-round economic development in the Near East. The Near East is supersensitive to the attachment of political strings to economic aid. Rightly or wrongly, people believe that economic aid is primarily a means for political appeasement, that is, for making certain sections of the Near East forget their political rights and claims. This suspicion ought to be effectively cleansed.

(12) Point Four for the most part aims at redressing economic and social injustice throughout the world. The noble motives behind this bold program will remain for generations an eloquent tribute to the generous American spirit of sharing one's knowledge, one's experience, one's technique, and one's wealth with the less developed, less experienced, less fortunate countries of the world. But as thus conceived Point Four is directed only to the means, conditions, frameworks, instruments of human existence. Surely this is not all that the United States can mean to itself and to the rest of the world. Surely this is not all that the United States is expected to mean to the Near East. Far more grievous than economic and social injustice is intellectual and spiritual injustice. There is the order of ends—what man should live for, what he should think, what he should believe, what he should be—about which the United States should have something to say, and concerning which it should have something significant and true to offer. It is for such contributions—contributions of the heart and the mind and the spirit—that the Near East thirsts. To give one an instrument without inducting him into communion with the whole spiritual culture which created that instrument in the first place, and without which it would be but a fetish and a fake, is utterly cruel and unjust. As long as there are millions of human beings in the Near East who have never tasted the infinite peace of mind and of reason, as long as the goods of the mind and spirit are deficient in our midst, as long as the great classics of human thought

22

and feeling, which have penetrated and transformed the life and literature and outlook of the West, are totally unheard of by large sections of the Near East, there can be no real prosperity and no genuine human well-being in that part of the world. I believe a sincere effort to render available to the peoples of the Near East, for their immediate use and in their own tongues, the finest classics of the West will be a potent factor in bringing about in the long run a genuine understanding between the Near East and the West.

VI

There are grave issues at stake in the world today, issues far graver than certain politicians imagine. For I believe what is in the balance today is nothing short of the highest spiritual values of the last four thousand years. Thus to try to conceive of how the Near East and the West may be brought closer together is an exceedingly serious matter. Who knows how much in the inscrutable course of events will depend on this? In the twelve-point concrete program I submit for consideration I have endeavored to be as positive, as practical, and as adequate as possible. There is nothing impracticable in what I say, provided only people understand and care.

Everything depends on the strength of the West, particularly intellectual and spiritual strength. Do you know why there are problems in the Near East?—because the West is not sure of itself. When the West comes back to its highest and rediscovers and reaffirms its best, our problems will be solved, and not ours alone. To that end, three things are needful: boldness, understanding, and love. To that end the Near East must be made to feel that it belongs.

When that happens, it is entirely possible that the Near East will move into a new golden period, whereby it will participate again in the creative arts of civilization. The great challenges facing it need not crush it: they may help to lift it onto a new level of being and achievement. Above all, its sons must learn how to put aside fruitless, hopeless suffering, which their fathers have known for generations, and how to put on the hopeful kind of suffering which, in joy, accepts everything for the sake of truth and being.

23

WILLIAM THOMSON

The Near East in the World

My subject is the Near East *in* the world, with some emphasis on the preposition "in"; and I propose to look at this question from the point of view of politics, pure and undefiled, undiluted, that is, by morality, which dilution according to a countryman of mine is the bane of modern liberal thought and action.

A wise old friend of mine once gave me some sage advice on building a sermon. Begin, he said to me, as far as possible from the lesson you wish to inculcate, then approach it circumspectly, and finally drive it home. My remarks on the *Near East in the World* may seem at first to be hewn too closely to my old friend's "canny" advice, but they are all relevant to our subject, I think, in the present circumstances of our world and will come at last to the point which I would make.

Human society with its culture and civilization and their instrument, the state, may, or may not, be subject to an organic necessity, a logic of time, which governs its birth, growth, and prime, its decay and death, as has been variously expounded by the Greek—Polybius—the Arab—Ibn Khaldun—the German—Spengler—and Mr. Toynbee of Princeton. But there are undoubtedly rhythmic sequences of events in history, which recur, varied indeed in their duration and in their distance in time from one another, but similar in their occasions and developments; and these sequences are well worth observing and studying, not only for the edification of students, but as patterns which may guide statesmen to wise actions. I would draw attention, then, to two at least of these sequences, as they affect our subject, the *Near East in the World,* as concisely as possible and therefore imperfectly, but nevertheless intelligibly, I hope.

24

THE NEAR EAST IN THE WORLD

Since the War of the Spanish Succession, at the beginning of the eighteenth century (1702–1713) at least, Great Britain's European policy has been governed by the principle that no single European power should dominate the continent of Europe, a policy condemned of late by some historians for various reasons, but a very judicious policy, which served the cause of liberty well in an imperfect world. In the Treaty of Utrecht (1713), which closed that war, England, it is true, recognized Philip of Anjou, grandson of Louis XIV of France, as king of Spain, in opposition to whose pretensions to that throne it had gone to war, but it did so only on condition that the French and Spanish crowns should never be united in one person.

For the very same reason, fear of French dominance in Europe, England entered the War of the Austrian Succession (1740–1748) on the side of Maria Theresa, whose claims to the throne it supported against those of the Elector of Bavaria, Charles, favored and backed by France and Prussia; and in the Napoleonic Wars (1796–1815) it allied itself in 1798 with Russia, Austria, Naples, Portugal, and the Ottoman Empire, and again in 1805 with Austria, Russia, and Sweden, and finally in 1815 with Russia, Austria, and Prussia, to meet and stay the perilous onrush of French arms under the Corsican adventurer; and during all this critical period England subsidized its allies, if not with the declared purpose of the Marshall Plan, at least with the same objective.

In the present century Britain has twice gone to war with Germany, urging a different *casus belli* each time, its treaties with Belgium and Poland, and proclaiming various ideal ends such as the security of small nations, but driven thereto by the same political motive, the preservation of its own freedom by aligning itself against any single power that threatened to dominate the continent of Europe. For such domination spelled for the British the loss of their freedom, with which in their eyes world-freedom was irrevocably linked; and so indeed in great measure it was. For if at that time any power could have overrun and held Europe, it would have gone ill with freedom's cause all over the world.

America entered the first World War and redressed the balance of power in Europe and so restored the equilibrium of the political world. But the end of the second World War finds the balance of power in the world teetering, largely because of the entry of a new factor, the awakening nationalism of Asiatic peoples, a development due in no small measure to the Asiatic policy of the United States based on the traditional American sentiment against imperialism and an undefined fervor for democracy, but lacking any clear-cut idea of the nature of the imperialism it would abolish, or of the conditions essential to the establishment of democracy in any nation, Asiatic, European, or American.

With the advent of Asiatic peoples into the circle of free, self-determining nations, and with their growing consciousness of their influence and power, the political scene has changed; and the problem which confronts the Western democracies now is how to prevent any single power from dominating, not just the continent of Europe, but the whole Eurasian continent; and America now plays the part that Great Britain filled in the eighteenth and nineteenth centuries. Russia, taught and probably now also advised by German geo-politicians, has recognized the changed political climate from the very beginning and did so possibly even during the war or before it, and has developed its world policy accordingly. American policy, on the other hand, up to the present at least, seems to have been based on the outworn nineteenth-century creed of the balance of power in Europe, equating that, as was then possible, with the equilibrium of the political forces of the world and overlooking, or miscalculating, the political potentialities of the Asiatic ferment. Europe is still, indeed, the most important factor in the political situation, but the awakening of Asia has upset the old scales of power. Its millions and resources represent an incalculable reservoir of men and material for the state which can control it either by orientation or regimentation.

Both scholars and statesmen have also misjudged the Asiatic situation in another particular at least. Up until the present, China has absorbed, as they put it, her conquerors. But these conquerors of the past were for the most part nomadic peoples in search of plenty with little civilization and less culture and not in any sense the missionaries and zealots of a new religion, or the bearers of a new way of life; and they were susceptible, therefore, to the more

26

advanced civilization of the conquered with its refinements and luxuries, its arts and crafts, and disposed also to accept and employ the educated classes of the old regime as teachers and administrators. A generation, or two at the most, saw the old culture proceed in its even way.

But the Communists advance with a new religion, or way of life, and a flaming zeal, and they have a quick and proven method of eliminating the classes that bear the old culture, believing and acting on the principle that control of all the educational facilities is the straight and narrow road to ultimate power and rule, a truth not altogether despised in the Western democracies, but which they have not acted upon, or cannot act upon, in their foreign relations. Over a century of British rule in India changed little of its culture, whatever progress in civilization may have been achieved. But a generation of communist rule will leave little of the old culture alive and productive.

Let us now approach nearer to the subject of this conference. From the dawn of history the same pattern, or sequence, of events has appeared again and again in what we call the Near East. In earliest recorded times (2900–1100 B.C.) we find a number of small states such as Beth-Eden, Gozan, Gurgum, Hattin, Hamath, and Damascus, standing side by side independent and free, whose destiny it was, however, to be subdued and dominated, or eliminated, by great empires east or west, Babylon, Egypt, the Hittites. But Babylon was overthrown by the Hittites, and Egyptian and Hittite power collapsed before the attacks of Lybians, the people of the North and the Sea and the Aramaeans (c. 1117); and then for three or four hundred years the peoples of the Near East enjoyed freedom from external pressure and control, small independent states arose again, Damascus, Ammon, Edom, Israel, Judea, etc., and the first flowering of native culture took place.

But in the ninth century B.C. there emerged in the east the powerful Assyrian empire, and its armies swept over the small states of the Near East and destroyed them: and when it fell in its turn, Babylon rose again and took its place (625–538 B.C.), to be succeeded by a rejuvenated Persia (538–332 B.C.).

Then out of the west came Alexander with his Macedonians on

his all-conquering march to India; and when he died (323 B.C.), the Ptolemies took over Egypt, and the Seleucids, Babylonia, and Syria (305–64/31 B.C.). For a brief interlude, however, during this period the Jews won and held their independence under the Maccabees (164–64 B.C.).

But from still further west advanced the legions of a still greater power, Rome; and at the end of the Third Mithridatic War (64 B.C.) Pompey made Syria a Roman province and put Judea under the authority of its governor: and from that time forth, from 36 B.C. until A.D. 642, the countries of the Near East became the frontier provinces of Rome and Parthia, Byzantium, and the Sassanian Empire, the battleground of their armies, and the spoil of the victor.

Meanwhile southward in Medina of the Hijaz Islam had been born, and in 632 the Arabs marched north and entered on that career of conquest that was to carry them west along North Africa to the Atlantic and into Spain and east to Transoxiana and India, and for the first time since ancient Babylon the Near East became again the hub of a world-empire with its capital at Damascus and later in Baghdad, an empire won and consolidated by the sword and a book, wherein grew and flourished a civilization and a culture that have sunk as deep and endured as long as those of Greece and Rome.

But the power of the Moslem Caliphate began to decline in the middle of the ninth century. Westward Egypt became then virtually independent under the Tulunids and later the Ikhshids, who both also ruled Syria (868–969), and in the tenth century under the Fatimids it was not only absolutely independent, but a rival Caliphate. Eastward one local dynasty after another seized the provinces of the Caliphate and established independent states, the Tahirids of Khorasan, the Saffarids of Persia (870–903), the Samanids of Transoxiana (872–999), the Buwayhids of Iraq and Persia (932–1055), the Ghaznawids of Afghanistan (962–1186). And it was in this period of the decay of the Caliphate, when East and West were both in turmoil, and no state, east or west, had the power to enforce its will far and wide, that the peoples of the Near East enjoyed again a brief interlude of uneasy and specious free-

28

dom, and small, independent states, or principalities, appeared again, the Hamdanids of Mosul and Aleppo (929–1003), the Mirdasids of Aleppo (1023–1079), the Uqaylids of Mosul (996–1096), the Marwanids of Diyar-Bakr (990–1096), and the Mazyadids of Hilla (1012–1032).

But in the next three centuries, the eleventh to the fourteenth, three successive waves of eastern invaders swept over the Near East, the Seljuks, the Mongols under Hulagu, and again under Timur. With the disintegration of the Seljuk empire in the middle of the twelfth century some small Turkish and Arab states were set up, the Burids of Damascus (1103–1154), the Zangids of Mesopotamia and Syria (1127–1250), and the Ortuqids of Diyar-Bakr (1101–1312); and the renowned Saladin incorporated part of Syria into his Sultanate of Egypt after his destruction of the Frankish Kingdom of Jerusalem. But these principalities all disappeared with the Mongol invasion of the latter half of the thirteenth century (1258–1260), or shortly thereafter, when only Egypt escaped the Mongol peril, saved by the great victory of the Mamelukes under Baybars at Ain Jalut (1260).

In the next century Timur and his Mongols almost destroyed the rising power of the Ottoman Turks at the battle of Angora (1402). But the Ottoman Empire survived this crushing defeat; and a little over a century later after consolidating its position in Europe it turned again south and east, overthrew the Mamelukes of Egypt, and annexed Egypt along with its Syrian possessions and the Hijaz with its two holy cities of Mecca and Medina (1517); and from that time until the first quarter of this century the Near East remained Turkish territory.

At the end of the first World War (1914–1918) the Turkish Empire was dismembered. By the Anglo-Russian-French agreement of April 26, 1916, and the Sykes-Picot Agreement between Great Britain and France of May 9, the Russians were to acquire Constantinople and the Straits, Armenia, part of Kurdistan, and Northern Anatolia westward from Trebizond to an undetermined point; the French were to receive the coastal strip of Syria, the Adana vilayet, Cilicia, and Southern Kurdistan with Kharput; and Britain was granted Mesopotamia and the ports of Haifa and

Acre in Syria. The rest of the Near East and Arabia were to be organized into an Arab state, or a federation of such states, divided into French and British spheres of influence, and Palestine was to have an international administration.

But the Bolshevik revolution of 1917, and the entry of America into the war, and the peace program published by the Western democracies with its proclamation of opportunity for the autonomous development of small nationalities and its guaranties of political independence and territorial integrity to great and small states alike seemed to change the whole political picture. In 1916 Great Britain had also promised the Grand Sherif of Mecca, Hussein, to recognize the independence of the Arab countries south of 37° N.L. and had in 1917 declared that it favored the establishment in Palestine of a national home for the Jewish people with some reservations. The stage was now set for another Near Eastern drama.

For once again we see in the Near East a group of small states, who owe their existence this time to the downfall of Tsarist Russia and to the weakness and rivalries of the two victorious European powers, but also, and as largely, to the idealism, however inept, and the sentiments of America. And again to the east, or northeast this time, and to the west of them lie great powers engaged in a seemingly inevitable struggle for world dominion, each—like Islam—with a book and a rule of life to win the souls of men, each with incalculable forces at their command.

How, then, stand the small states of the Near East? Their value and importance to the contending powers rest almost wholly upon the strategic situation of their land and upon some economic resources, oil especially. To one of these powers they are a gateway to the Mediterranean and Africa; to its rivals they are a bulwark, however insecure, of their lines of communication. At present they are buffer states, but, if the cold war turns hot, they will become a no-man's land.

Undoubtedly the Western book with its plan of salvation and program of coöperation is more agreeable, if not also more intelligible, to the peoples of the Near East, Moslem, Jew, or Christian, than the rigid, leveling gospel from the East. But they fear, and justly so, that the Western democracies will not be able, or even willing, to defend them if hostilities begin and that they will be sacrificed for time in the Western strategy. They themselves are negligible in respect of power; and not only are they weak in themselves, they are also hopelessly divided, the one against the other, each persisting in a particularistic policy in almost utter disregard of the ominous world situation.

The Arabs are also disaffected towards the Western allies, with some reason it must be confessed. Communistic cells are reported from Lebanon, Syria, and Iraq, and Israel and Egypt also are not untouched by the world-wide virus. Peasants, the dispossessed, and the unemployed are always subject to such infections in unsettled times. Israel and Egypt, as their actions show, would also avoid, if possible, any commitments or entanglements, a policy speciously attractive for the moment.

Arab idealists look back regretfully to the golden era of Damascus and Baghdad and would recall that era in a modern guise as far as possible, but first they must overcome the intransigent particularism of their peoples and leaders. Jewish idealists recall with yearning the glory that was Israel and would create it anew. The wit of man might be able to resolve the inherent improbabilities of this situation given the opportunity. But the times are out of joint. We do not live in a period in which the balance of power in the world is such as to grant small states the grace to live at peace between or among strong states and be free to develop according to their own light and will. It is an era of explosive ideas and expanding forces, Babylon versus Egypt again, Rome versus Persia, Alexander again, or Islam; and willy-nilly, small states must choose one side or the other and prepare themselves for the issue, or remain outside any system of defense, a fair and easy prey for either side.

In the present chaotic and unsettled conditions of the Near East states, the West must consider them as one of the weakest, if also one of the most crucial, links in its chain of defense and act accordingly. For some basis of unity is imperative, if any front at all is to be made against an invader; and without that front the lines of communication of the Western democracies with their Eastern

31

allies and dependencies are broken perhaps irretrievably. These states lie on the flank and to the rear of Turkey and Greece, at present the West's two forward bastions in its system of defense in this area, and with Iran they offer to the Red Power the easiest access to the Mediterranean, and the Indian Ocean, and beyond.

The prospect is not bright. But the leaders of the Near East states and the statesmen of the West have had time and warning enough to forecast future eventualities and to do what even yet may be done to prepare their peoples not only by word, but also by act, for whatever may be in store for them. The sad truth is, however, that most politicians have a blind eye for the lessons of history, since in the party-programs and on the political hustings of democracy these lessons have neither the local interest nor the popular attraction so necessary today for the gaining and keeping of political power, however necessary they may be for wise and prudent political action.

HARVEY P. HALL

The Pattern of Great Power Impact on the Near East

It has become something of a cliché to remark that the strategic interests of the world powers converge upon the Near East, even as do the continents themselves. The importance of the Black Sea straits and the Suez Canal, of Turkey and Iran, as water and land bridges from north to south and west to east is readily apparent to anyone who takes the trouble to glance at a map. There is no particular need to be coached in Great Britain's "historic lifeline to India," or in Russia's "search for a warm water outlet," or in imperial Germany's *Drang nach Osten* to appreciate the geopolitical problems the Near East is forced to face. As if to reinforce the accidents of surface geography, the Near East's vast resources of oil assure the continued concern of all major powers in its welfare.

The conflicting nature of these interests of the powers is the aspect normally emphasized by those considering the importance of the Near East. We are prone to approach the area not out of direct interest in it as the locale of living nations, but as the arena of an international struggle. We tend to overlook the pattern of great power activity, and the benefit which the Near East might derive therefrom if it were shrewd enough to do so. For whereas the tactics of the powers differ and all too frequently do conflict, their ultimate aims are remarkably similar. In short, each of the great powers directly concerned in the Near East—Great Britain, France, the United States, and the Soviet Union—desires that the countries and peoples of the area be stable and friendly. The conflicts and differences arise from the tactics used that these twin aims may be achieved; the degree of conflict being in direct proportion, of course, with the degree of conflict among the powers themselves.

In analyzing the tactics that each of the great powers has employed to create a Near East which is at once stable and friendly, it is possible to make the generalization that each has fallen back upon that element of its own political philosophy in which it has the greatest faith. This generalization, like all such, demands qualification, but not to the extent that the resulting pattern is hard to trace.

The political faith of Great Britain is founded upon its constitution. So long as King and Parliament stand, there will always be an England. It was only natural, therefore, that when the British began to relinquish direct political control of the Arab states—their protectorate over Egypt and their mandates over Transjordan and Iraq (Palestine was a special case)—they attempted to endow them with British-type political structures and a faith in British-type political institutions. As additional insurance that these countries would proceed along a path that was straight and friendly, Britain tied them to her with treaties endowing her with special influence.

The attempt was only partially successful for a number of reasons. British political institutions are the product of a long historical evolution; together with the form they have assumed have grown up deeply rooted traditions. The British parliament developed out of a struggle to limit the power of the vested central authority, first of the nobility against the king, then of the middle class against the aristocracy, and finally of the common man against the well-to-do. Among the countries of the Near East, the present parliaments of only Iran and Turkey can possibly claim to be born out of any such struggle. In Iran the Majlis and Constitution of 1906 came into being as a means of restricting the arbitrary and ruinating power of the Shah. Whereas in England the struggle for power among the Commons and the Lords and the King has been left behind in the process of constitutional evolution, it is still quite apparent in Iran. In Turkey this particular struggle dropped suddenly out of sight with the declaration of the Republic by the Kemalists in 1923.

In none of the Arab countries which were endowed with British-inspired constitutions was there any natural evolution pointing toward such political structures. On the contrary, the complete form of government was created by fiat: ruling dynasty, upper house, and lower house. Little or no tradition existed to give it meaning. Also lacking was any tradition of the British concept of the political party, without which the British system fails to function.

The British were, in fact, being more faithful to the form of their political institutions than to their essence. But what has endowed England with stability is not the form of its political institutions so much as its faith in political evolution. In passing on their political structure to the Near East, the British were not attempting to build security on this basic principle. On the contrary, they were attempting in this fashion to freeze the social structure of the state in its then current form, partly in the hope that their own position could thus be maintained. What they passed on was largely artificial and static, and sure to prove itself weak when faced with the dynamics of a rising and turbulent nationalism.

In contrast to the British, the French evidence little faith in the efficacy of their political institutions. This is more than offset, however, by their profound faith in the invincibility of French culture. Constitutions, assemblies, and premiers may come and go, but so long as the tradition of French culture remains, there will always be a France. They also feel convinced that any people which has caught hold of the clear beauty of French *belles lettres* and the rationality of French thought must perforce be sympathetic toward France and have the strength to override political or social upheavals. It is not remarkable, therefore, that France has chosen this line above all others to forward its position in the Near East.

Several factors have favored France in this approach. During the latter years of the eighteenth century the Moslem East began to open itself to influence from the West. The need to do so was borne in upon it by the realization—chiefly following the disastrous defeat which the Ottoman Empire sustained in 1774, following one of its periodic wars with Russia—of the extent to which the West had pulled ahead in military power. The Napoleonic Wars drew the Ottoman Empire directly into the European arena of conflict.

In 1798 a French army under Napoleon invaded Egypt and marched into Syria, only to be expelled by a British force, allied to the Turks, in 1801. A combined Russian-Turkish fleet captured the Ionian Islands from the French in 1799, and for a time Russian warships were permitted to pass the Turkish Straits in order to supply this Mediterranean base. In 1807 a British fleet, attempting to counteract a rebirth of French influence at the Porte, forced the Straits in the opposite direction and stood off Constantinople for ten days, alternately negotiating and threatening attack. Drawn first to Napoleon's side by his fantastic military successes, then swung to the other by the threats of Great Britain and Russia, the Porte was caught in the tangle of European power politics, and the Eastern Question of the nineteenth century was born.

The Turks, in their attempt to learn the secret of European power, quite naturally turned toward the French. France was Turkey's oldest ally in Europe. Napoleon's struggle with Russia—Turkey's most feared enemy—offset the shock of his abortive invasion of Egypt, whereas Great Britain's alliance with Russia tended to weaken its influence in this period. Turkey was primarily anxious to learn the secret of Western military science, and who had demonstrated its mastery with more effect than the French?

As contact with the West broadened in the first half of the nineteenth century to include cultural as well as technical association, it was still natural that the Moslem East should turn to France for its major inspiration. During the eighteenth century, French culture had become the dominant culture of continental Europe; the writings of the French rationalists were the end product of Western thought. Here was the philosophy of the West presented in neat bundles. It was thus far easier for the Moslem, accustomed to having all life reduced to a system, to grasp the content and form of French culture than, for example, the more amorphous Anglo-Saxon. He could appreciate the codification of law far more readily than the evolution of common law from a bewildering progression of precedents. Thus matching the faith of the Frenchman in the power of his culture to persuade was a readiness on the part of the Near Easterner to receive. As a result, French contact with the East has had a more Europeanizing effect than that of any other.

But unfortunately for France's influence in the area, an affection for its culture did not prepare the ground for a parallel affection for its politics. When France assumed the mandates over Lebanon and Syria after World War I, it had a sound basis for success in the former and at least an even chance in the latter. But France's assumption that the Lebanese and Syrians, out of love for French culture and a sentimental attachment to France's "historic" role in the Levant, would become willing servants of French interests was wide of the mark. Before the mandatory period came to an end during the course of World War II, France had well-nigh lost all the prestige it had previously acquired, cultural as.well as political. It is interesting to note that France, both in its retreat from the scene and in its attempts to reëstablish iself since then, has again put faith in the power of its national culture in the firm belief that even though its armies were defeated, its navy destroyed, its territory invaded, its body politic split asunder in civil war, and much of its empire lost or in revolt, the basic qualities which have given France its character in the past cannot die. In the latter years of the war, when France realized that its political and military withdrawal from Lebanon and Syria was imminent, a last-resort attempt was made to persuade former mandates to sign a convention assuring French language and culture a preëminent position in the Lebanese and Syrian educational systems. The attempt failed, but in the years since then France has not abandoned the effort to keep its prestige alive through cultural activity. With the taint of persuasion by force removed, the leaven of French culture is again free to act.

The United States, in its approach to the Near East, has taken still a third tack. Although Americans profess a belief in democracy, they have never shown much missionary spirit in spreading it abroad. Certainly American political institutions are so peculiarly a result of the unique composition of the United States that there has never been much faith in their suitability for peoples of other cultures. Nor has American culture produced a way of life which can be preached abroad as a universal philosophy.

The faith of the average American is built more than anything else on two foundations: Christian ethics and a higher standard of material living. Translated into a policy to assure that the nations of the Near East be both stable and friendly to the United States, this means an effort to make Near Easterners at once more virtuous (in a rather puritanical sense) and economically well off.

The century or more of American activity in the Near East which preceded World War II did not represent a conscious attempt to forward a national policy, but nevertheless reflected these basic American beliefs. This activity was largely educational, and had a twofold aim: the "building of men," and the endowing of them with a practical training which would enable them both to improve their own well-being and the well-being of those around them; in the Biblical words of the motto of the American University of Beirut: "that they may have life and have it more abundantly." Thus the emphasis of American education has been upon the training of doctors, educators, economists, and so forth, rather than upon an understanding of the mainsprings of Christian and Moslem, Western and Eastern culture. This is in marked contrast to the type of emphasis one finds, for example, at the French Université de St. Joseph, also in Beirut. In part because of its intrinsic value, and in part because it was conducted entirely through private, non-propagandistic agencies, this American educational tradition was extraordinarily successful in building, among Near Easterners, a friendly feeling for the United States, even if it did portray the United States more as it liked to believe itself to be than as it actually was.

When the United States began to develop a national policy toward the Near East following World War II, it set out to continue in this tradition. Politically, the countries of the area were to be free of their prewar mentors. Independence must come to Lebanon, Syria, and a partitioned Palestine; the integrity of Greece, Turkey, and Iran must be maintained against Soviet aggression. But once these matters were settled, the long-range accent was to be upon cultural exchange and technical assistance in projects to develop the area economically, to give the common people better health and the means for greater productivity, to point the way toward more efficient administration. If the people could be well fed, clothed, and housed, their governments would be stable and they themselves contented, grateful, and friendly. This is the principle behind our sponsorship of the Point Four program, and of the United Nations Economic Survey Mission in the fall of 1949.

Unfortunately for the United States, this primarily economic approach to the Near East has been complicated by continuing political factors in which it has been forced to take a hand; nor does it take into account the very basic fact that when it comes to politics, the Arab does not live by bread alone. Officially, the United States favored the partition of Palestine into Jewish and Arab states in order to bring the territory independence with the greatest possible speed and fairness and resultant degree of stability. But the manner in which its Palestine policy was carried out conveyed the strong impression, at least to the Arab nations, that the United States' real objective was the creation of a Jewish state at all cost. United States policy also appeared to them to be a denial of the principles of political democracy—primarily that of the right of self-determination—in which they had been taught Americans believed. The result was a loss of a large part of their traditional good will toward the United States and of all confidence in any future undertaking it might sponsor. Fears of exploitation by American business, the sensing of ulterior motives in any scheme to assist the Palestine refugees, doubts as to the wisdom of accepting American support in a technical assistance program—such characterize the current relations between the Arab countries and the United States. Its repercussion on world affairs may be seen in the Arab reaction to United Nations intervention in Korea, which hasn't changed.

We turn, finally, to the pattern of Soviet policy in the Near East. The collapse of Tsarist Russia during World War I, and the repudiation, by the Bolsheviks, of all Tsarist expansionist tactics wiped the slate clean for a fresh Russian approach. The communist doctrine pointed naturally to penetration of the area through an attack upon its social structure, rather than through the old-fashioned type of imperialism. It soon became apparent, however, that the new tactics were serving ends not far different from the old. They had both their negative and their positive aspects: first, to break the position which the Western powers, particularly Great Britain, enjoyed in the area; second, to build up native communist movements in each of the countries—movements which would eventually revolutionize Near East societies and draw them into the Soviet orbit. When one asserts, therefore, that the Soviet Union, like the other Great Powers, wants a Near East which is friendly and stable, one does not mean a Near East stabilized in its present form, but rather only after it has been softened up and rendered receptive to communism.

The Soviet Union's tactics have been most clearly revealed in Iran, the only Near Eastern country to date where it has felt that the native communist movement had progressed sufficiently to favor an attempt to take over the whole country. But the 1946 Azerbaijan crisis proved abortive, the threatened coup in Teheran never came off, and the Iranian communist movement was driven underground. In Turkey, attempts at communist infiltration have come up against a long tradition of national pride and a deep-rooted fear, reaching down to the common people, of all things Russian. Recent attempts to force an entry into the country through a revised Straits Convention granting the Soviet Union the right to maintain bases on Turkish territory, and through asserting claims to Turkey's eastern provinces—both moves supported by a bitter press and radio campaign calculated to undermine the Turks' faith in their own government—have been to no avail. In the Arab countries, the Soviet approach has been through appeals to the growing labor class, to potentially powerful minority groups, and to younger elements in the population dissatisfied with the inefficiency and corruption of the present regimes. The Kremlin's efforts have been extremely successful in undermining the strength of the British and American position, and in raising thereby the U.S.S.R.'s own prestige in comparison; they have been less so in the positive attempt to build communist sentiment among the Arabs, although the native communist movements, fed largely on lack of respect for the current regimes, must never be underestimated.

Each of the major powers has thus tended to follow its own bent in its attempt to establish a firm footing in the Near East: Great Britain through the introduction of political institutions looking to parallel British institutions for inspiration; France through implanting a love for all things French; the United States through providing the means for a more comfortable material life; the Soviet Union through social revolution designed to make the common people feel that power is theirs—the political, cultural, economic, and social approaches. The picture, of course, is not so simple as this, for each of the powers has at times used other means as well. Certainly, Great Britain has had a tremendous influence over the economic development of the Near East, particularly in Egypt and the Sudan; France has experimented with the direct political approach, most recently in its administration of the mandates of Lebanon and Syria; the United States has been involved, since World War II, in the political evolution of Palestine, in preserving the independence of Iran and Turkey, and in establishing that of Syria and Lebanon; also, possibly a very superficial "American" culture may be said to have spread throughout the area. The U.S.S.R.'s basically social approach has certainly been qualified by political and cultural penetration, and direct military intervention. Nevertheless, the generalization would appear to hold that the most lasting effect of each power's impact is along the line of the major element in its policy. Which of these means of approach is likely to prove the most effective in forwarding the interests of the powers is not the point of discussion here, but rather what, taken together, their net effect on the Near East is likely to be.

It has become a habit to deplore the effects of Western imperialism. No doubt many of its motives and tactics have been deplorable, since they were designed, primarily, to service the interests of the initiator and not of the subject. They involved economic exploitation, as is witnessed by the terms of concession agreements concluded in the past, by France's economic policy in Syria and Lebanon, and by Britain's policy in Egypt and the Sudan. They involved political manipulation, for which numerous illustrations may be drawn from the administration of the mandates, and the sequence of political crises in Egypt, Iraq, and Iran. They brought forced involvement in foreign strategic plans, and in wars of which the peoples of the Near East were innocent, cultural bewilderment, and social strain and upheaval.

On the other hand, the process has brought the Near East into direct contact with many of the best attributes of Western civilization: practical experience with its political institutions, insight into its leading cultures, training in its techniques, and exposure to its social ideologies. The composite of Big Power contact with the Near East has presented a fairly complete pattern of Western civilization, the civilization which is by all odds dominant in the world today and must be at least partially absorbed if any people is to survive. The West has given the East much constructive material on which to build, if it can be seen clearly, and free from false motivations. The question now is whether the unfortunate aspects of Western penetration will so dominate the Near Easterners' thoughts and emotions that no benefit can accrue; or whether the East can sift out the seeds of value—something of Britain's political faith, something of France's graceful rationalism, something of America's techniques, even something of the Soviet Union's declared faith in the common man—and use them in synthesizing a modern East-West culture of its own. If the East borrows merely what is materially attractive, without learning the spirit of constant questioning and experimenting which has brought Western Civilization into being and gives it life, the East will never build this modern culture. But if it can take those things from the West which can be attuned to the durable elements in its own heritage, the net result of the impact may be the laying of the foundation for a renewed, vigorous, and genuinely native culture.

At present it is impossible to say what turn this process will take. It depends on what elements of current Near Eastern culture prove to be dominant—whether Islamic thinking, for example, will develop along sectarian lines, or whether it will rediscover something of the universality of its classic period. It also depends on which element of the West, the democratic or totalitarian, comes to dominate European and American—and Asiatic—political life.

GEORGE G. McGHEE

Economic Development and the Near East

Throughout the Near East, as indeed throughout the remainder of the vast underdeveloped areas of the world, people are impelled by a basic reality—the fact of poverty amid potential plenty. Daily in their press and in their parliaments, and in every international conference they attend, they are demanding an improvement in their way of life.

A billion or more people today live in countries where the average income per person is less than $100 a year, compared with our average of about $1400. Today these masses are awakening to the realization that they are not sharing in the world's progress. They know that their countries have resources which can be developed— land that could yield more food for hungry mouths; minerals, oil, and timber for development; rivers for irrigation or power.

In these countries successive generations have taken it for granted that poverty was their lot, that no way of progress was open to them. Now they refuse to continue being fatalists. Now they know that it is possible for them to enjoy, if not riches, at least a standard of living progressively nearer to what is decent and tolerable. They know that we and other economically advanced countries have found means of applying human energies to the resources of nature, means of organizing economic life for the benefit of our peoples. They want to develop their own potentialities, and they intend to find means of doing so.

The countries of the Near East are in many ways typical of the world's underdeveloped nations. I have recently visited all of these countries. I have talked with their leaders. I have seen how strong is their desire for economic progress, how anxious they are to receive the kind of help which we are uniquely equipped to offer.

43

Obviously it is in our own interest that they develop along economic lines. Our greatest trade is with the more developed countries. We cannot, moreover, hope to protect our own vital interests in peace, freedom, and economic progress in a world of poverty. The underdeveloped countries share our objectives. It is in our interest to help them to achieve sufficient economic strength and political stability to be effective partners in the common task of establishing a peaceful world.

If, then, it is in our interest to support the drive for economic development over vast areas of the world, it will be worth our while to examine what countries such as those of the Near East are doing to promote their own progress; what difficulties they are encountering; and what we have done and can do to assist them. Although we are concerned principally with the Near East, any conclusions we reach are applicable in large measure to all the underdeveloped countries of the world.

When we examine existing development programs in different countries, our first impression is one of great diversity. In some cases we find countries whose peoples have only a vision of economic progress and a longing for its achievement. Some lack the knowledge or the will to begin. Other countries have formulated and are attempting to carry out comprehensive programs. Many have reached the point where they are just beginning to realize how great a task they have undertaken.

There is also great diversity in the extent to which the ingredients of economic development are at hand. One such ingredient is the foreign exchange with which to buy raw materials, agricultural and industrial equipment, and technical services. Some of the countries of the Near East have always been able to earn foreign exchange through sales of their own raw materials, such as cotton from Egypt and oil from Saudi Arabia, Iraq, and Iran. Other states, however, earn almost no foreign exchange, since they are unable to generate an excess of exports over imports.

The position of these latter countries must seem to them like an unbreakable closed circle. They cannot produce any significant volume of goods for export unless they can import the necessary tools and techniques, but they cannot earn enough to pay for imported tools and techniques because of their low productivity. Such countries are constantly plagued by the problem of finding foreign financial assistance—a problem to which I shall return in a later context.

I have been thinking in general terms and about groups or classes of countries. Let me give a few concrete examples.

You have no doubt heard about the Iranian seven-year development program. In the past, the free play of economic forces failed to result in sufficient economic progress in Iran. Accordingly, the Government of Iran, on its own initiative and motivated by its genuine desire to better the condition of its peoples, decided to apply to the economic development of the country the bulk of the Government's oil revenues. In order to make the best use of these funds, the Government hired a group of American engineering firms in an advisory capacity.

This group studied not only the native resources of the country, but the various facilities in existence—roads, railroads, ports, sources of power, and so on. It also examined the sources of domestic savings within Iran, the supply of labor skills, and the adequacy of the administrative machinery of the Government to direct the application of the human resources to the natural endowments of the country.

As a result of this study, the Iranians have prepared the groundwork for a balanced program of development. They have already found, however, that they have many problems which cannot be solved quickly, and many which money alone cannot solve. They have found serious limiting factors, such as inadequate administration, and lack of skilled personnel, which have thus far slowed their program. In short, Iran has learned how big a job economic development is—how difficult it is for a country to lift itself by its economic bootstraps.

The case of Turkey is interesting from quite a different point of view. In Turkey also, the Government took the economic initiative. The new Republic, which was established in 1923, embarked on a program of Westernization and industrialization under the inspired leadership of its founder, Kemal Atatürk.

That program has been pursued with vigor and determination,

45

and the progress which has been achieved during the past 27 years has been most impressive. But it is particularly significant, I feel, that Turkey's concept of how its economic development could be accomplished most effectively has changed in recent years.

In the early days of the Republic, its leaders wanted to make up for lost time in reaching the economic levels of the more advanced Western countries. But at that time there were in Turkey virtually no domestic savings; there was no tradition of private risk-taking; there was little managerial or technical skill; and there was little chance to attract foreign capital for development projects. Fearing that the desired rate of economic development could not be carried on by the private enterprise system then existing, the Government decided that the state should take the lead in the economic field.

Although Turkey has, under this system of state capitalism, made considerable progress in developing its industrial plant, there has been growing recognition in recent years that such a system will not best achieve full utilization of the country's resources. Many state industries were inefficient by Western standards. Many were a drain on the Government, rather than an asset, and were forced to charge excessive prices for their products. Evidence of this recognition lies in the Turkish Government's announcement in the summer of 1950 that it intends to reduce state intervention in economic life to a minimum, to narrow the scope of state economic enterprise, and to broaden, as far as possible, the field of private enterprise. It also expressed its intention gradually to transfer to private enterprise, as conditions might permit, many economic enterprises now operated by the state.

A further manifestation of this recognition lies in the creation, during 1950, with the encouragement of the Turkish Government, of the Industrial Development Bank. Its capital has been subscribed by private Turkish interests. In addition to loan funds which it can mobilize in Turkey, the bank expects to obtain additional funds in foreign exchange from the International Bank for Reconstruction and Development, and to lend these funds to private Turkish citizens and companies for the establishment of industrial enterprises in that country.

These cases bring out, I think, some of the difficulties confront-

46

ing any country aspiring to development. Since Turkey and Iran are among the more advanced countries of the Near East, many other countries can expect equal or greater difficulties.

Perhaps the most fundamental obstacle to economic progress is the absence of basic resources, a lack of the needed ingredients of economic development in the right place at the right time. For example, minerals and fuels, even though present, may not have been fully exploited, and existing power capacity may be inadequate to permit introduction of desirable improvements in industrial technique. In other cases, where the required raw materials and power supplies exist, transport facilities may be inadequate to carry the products of industry to a market large enough to support it. In still other cases, the energies of too large a part of the population are being expended in extracting food supplies from arid land by inept methods of cultivation. In all these situations, the difficulty is that of determining where to start in providing the required resources.

Closely akin to the obstacle posed by the lack of basic resources is that of the absence of suitable institutions. This fundamental difficulty in countries like those of the Near East is one which we in this country find it difficult to visualize. When someone here wants to start a new business, he takes it for granted that there is a bank with which he can discuss his financial problems. He takes it for granted that there are a labor market and labor exchanges through which he can assemble the various skills which he will need. He takes it for granted that he can arrange for any necessary insurance against the hazards of fire, flood, or injury to his employees, simply by picking up the telephone.

He takes it for granted that he can, with virtually no effort and at slight cost, establish a business corporation as the organizational form for his enterprise. He can safely assume that the legal status of all contracts into which he may enter will be determinate and will be protected by the courts. He can assume that there are at his command almost all kinds of transport facilities; he knows he can hire or buy trucks if his proposed plant is not located near a rail line or a deep-water port. He takes it for granted that if a truck breaks down he can find a mechanic to fix it.

It is therefore difficult for us to picture a situation in which banking facilities frequently consist of little more than money lenders' private shops; in which insurance coverage can be obtained, if at all, only by arduous negotiations with an overseas insurance organization; in which there are no real labor exchanges and it is even more difficult to find a mechanic to fix a truck than to find the truck in the first place; in which required facilities cannot be hired because they do not exist.

A third problem in the underdeveloped Near Eastern countries arises from the shortage of technical and managerial skills. It is obvious that there can be no great supply of high-level business administration talent in a country which has no tradition of large-scale business enterprise. In many countries of the Near East, 90 per cent of the so-called industrial establishments are small handicraft shops employing not over eight or ten workmen. Lack of administrative talent, however, is not the most pressing problem. As the scale of business operations increases, administrative skills will presumably develop as needed.

An even greater obstacle, however, is the lack of suitable technical and professional talent. Even in countries such as Turkey, where an intensive effort has been made to train a generation of industrial engineers by sending intelligent young men abroad for technical studies, there is a tendency for the engineers so trained to be divorced from the actual operation of industrial processes. In many countries, the foreign-trained engineer tends to think of himself as a professional man and becomes a white-collar engineer. It would not occur to some of them to put on hip boots and work gloves and go out to supervise a job in muck and dirt; too often that is left to an untrained assistant. Also, foreign-trained specialists tend to think and plan in terms of the elaborate technical organization that characterizes the industry of the United States or Germany or the country in which they were trained, even though such an organization may not be applicable to their own countries.

Another related problem is the serious lack of personnel of the shop foreman or field manager type. Between unskilled labor and the various categories of moderately skilled artisans, on the one hand, and the foreign-trained specialists, on the other, a major gap frequently exists. The problem here is partly one of education and partly one of developing a sounder concept of how production should be organized.

Another problem—and this primarily a matter of attitudes—is the lack of a spirit or instinct for risk-taking. Those who have wealth seek the safest forms of investment for it. They enlarge their land holdings or acquire precious metals and gems. Others invest in quick-turnover speculations which leave no residue of improved productive plant, no legacy of long-range economic benefit to the community.

Finally, in some countries, the structure of political and social institutions either provides no incentive to economic innovation or actively discourages it. For instance, in countries where the code of business law is relatively new, business organization and business contracts tend to assume forms which conform to the existing code, even though such forms may not be well suited to the progressive evolution of economic activity. A more important limiting factor, in many underdeveloped countries, is the system of land tenure, which provides no incentive to increase agricultural productivity. Where the great mass of the agricultural population consists of tenants under absentee landlords, there is no incentive for the tenant-farmer to invest in farm buildings, irrigation facilities, terracing, or other lasting improvements. Rigid adherence to old customs, such as the African practice of regarding the number of cattle owned as a symbol of one's wealth, without reference either to the productivity of cattle or its relationship to grass lands, stultifies economic progress.

All the foregoing obstacles to economic development are of such a character that they cannot be overcome by the mere expenditure of money. They arise out of existing social attitudes or existing institutions, which must be changed if progress is to be made. This is not to say, however, that lack of money—lack of capital—is not itself a major deterrent to economic progress.

In the first place, there are in most of the countries of the Near East almost no usable domestic savings. Of the small volume of savings which is accumulated, the bulk goes out of the country. While foreign borrowing and the import of capital are very important aids to economic progress, no large or lasting development can be expected unless the community itself can develop a capacity to save and to put its savings to use in expanding industrial and agricultural plants. Here again we encounter the same closed-circle problem, since the capacity to save depends on the ability to produce more than enough for subsistence. If productivity cannot be increased, net savings cannot be accumulated. Even assuming, however, that productivity can be increased either through borrowing abroad or through adoption of new techniques of production, or both, there still remains the problem of mobilizing the saving potential thus created. That problem, as you know, has been solved in our own country by an almost bewildering diversity of savings institutions. Few, if any, of these institutions now exist in such countries as Egypt or Iraq, for example.

Second, the problem of finding foreign financial assistance is also acute. A country seeking economic development can seek funds from abroad, generally speaking, through any or all of three different channels: public or intergovernmental lending; borrowing on the private capital markets of the world; and the inflow of direct private investment. There are limits at the present time on the extent to which these channels are available to the underdeveloped areas.

The agencies capable of providing intergovernmental loans are few in number, with relatively small resources. The Export-Import Bank, an American Government lending agency, can make and has made loans to underdeveloped areas. The main purpose, however, of the Export-Import Bank is to finance projects leading to the promotion of American export or import trade. Furthermore, the bank's resources form a revolving fund which must be committed primarily to ventures which offer good prospects for repayment in dollars within a reasonable period of time. Projects designed to cope with the closed-circle problem of the underdeveloped countries, by the very nature of the problem, would have at best an uncertain chance of generating their own means of repayment in the short run.

The International Bank for Reconstruction and Development has great possibilities as a lending and financing agency. At the present time, however, the bank's lendable resources are small, relative to what they may ultimately be, and the bank has only limited authority to lend in currencies other than the dollar. Furthermore, the Articles of Agreement of the bank require it to observe approximately the same criteria regarding likelihood of repayment as those which govern the Export-Import Bank, and therefore it presents the same difficulties as a means of helping underdeveloped countries to overcome their closed-circle position. It is important to bear this in mind.

The governments of other economically advanced countries are not now in a position to undertake more than a nominal amount of intergovernmental lending. Countries such as Britain and France, for example, have large capital requirements for reconstruction and expansion of industry at home, as well as development responsibilities in their dependencies.

Borrowing on the private capital markets of the world is, unhappily, almost an extinct phenomena, at least for the time being. I understand that the total volume of foreign loans floated in the New York bond market since the end of World War II does not exceed 25 million dollars. In other countries, because of the intense need for capital at home, foreign bond flotations are also at a minimum, except for some small issues placed in Switzerland and certain dominion and colonial issues placed in London.

Turning to the availability of direct private investment, there has been a substantial amount of foreign investment since the end of the war by American oil companies. If this investment activity, which represents quite a special case, is excluded, the volume of direct private investment taking place now is disappointingly small, amounting to less than 300 million dollars per year to the whole world outside the United States.

There are, of course, many reasons for this, among which the currency situation is the paramount difficulty. American companies are understandably hesitant to make large investments abroad when the chances of amortizing their investment and bringing home the profit of such investment are problematic. This difficulty is increased because those American concerns which might normally be interested in making foreign investments have large opportunities to expand their domestic plants and operations and in doing so to make a good return in dollars. Beyond this basic currency difficulty, there are other deterrents, such as the unsatisfactory state of our commercial treaty relations with many of those countries, or, in certain cases, the existence of laws discriminating against foreign investors.

It may sound as if I have been reeling off a catalogue of insurmountable obstacles. They are not insurmountable. In our own country we surmounted them. With the help of our leadership, the underdeveloped areas can overcome them. What have we been providing in the way of leadership? What is the content of our contribution to economic development abroad?

I have already alluded to some things we have done. We have, for example, expanded the authorized capital of the Export-Import Bank and have made a number of development loans, largely in Latin America, but including some eight loans in the Near Eastern and African areas. Our Government has also provided the bulk of available loan funds to the International Bank for Reconstruction and Development, which has, for example, recently advanced funds to India and Iraq. Additionally, I might observe, the private capital market of the United States has absorbed 250 million dollars of the bonds of the International Bank, increasing its loanable funds by that amount. We have also participated extensively in the financing of the other specialized agencies of the United Nations, such as the World Health Organization and the Food and Agriculture Organization, which have begun to make significant contributions to economic development.

Our best-known undertaking, however, has been in the development of the Point IV Program. Point IV is a major step forward. Under this program, as it has been authorized by the Congress, we can make technical experts available to the underdeveloped countries. Let me give a few examples of what can be done in this regard. The Food and Agriculture Organization has two veterinarians working now in Ethiopia inoculating cattle against rinderpest, at the rate of 10,000 cattle per month. This means that, at a cost of a few cents per head of cattle, it is possible to save

Ethiopian farmers thousands of dollars and greatly to improve the diet of the people of Ethiopia. Similarly, under the United States Economic Mission to Liberia, American farm experts have for some years been at work improving the quality and quantity of food production. Last year Liberia, for the first time, was able to produce its total requirements of rice, its staple food.

We can also, under Point IV, bring trainees from the underdeveloped areas to this country so that they can themselves acquire specialized knowledge and skills. There are already many agricultural students from the Near East in our Western agricultural schools. If, under Point IV, more of them can come, the end result may well be a change in the whole concept of agriculture as it is now practiced in the Near East.

It must be remembered, however, that neither the American Government's Point IV program nor the United Nations' Technical Assistance Program is designed to solve the problem of external finance. Neither the United States nor the United Nations will provide funds for the establishment of industries, or for the construction of roads and dams. These programs are designed merely to facilitate the flow of technical knowledge. Under our Point IV Program, in short, we will export technicians and specialists; we will not export capital. I do not imply that our Point IV Program is too small. I am merely emphasizing that it is not a complete approach to the problem of economic development. It is not intended to be. It tackles the technical interchange problem.

I have reviewed the nature and the content of the world-wide drive for economic development. I have reviewed some, but by no means all of the obstacles to be overcome on the road to economic development. And I have briefly reviewed what is being done to promote economic development.

In the light of what we have seen, can we expect to see rapid progress in the Near East and other underdeveloped areas? I wish I could answer yes categorically, but in all probability progress will be much slower than the United States and the underdeveloped areas would wish. This is unavoidable. However, the real tragedy would arise if progress were to be less rapid than it could be and should be. Here is the challenge, both to the underdeveloped areas and to ourselves.

The challenge to us is the challenge of providing leadership, with all that word implies. To provide leadership means to know what needs to be done, to know how it should be done, to recognize the difficulties and means of overcoming them, and, above all, to instill into the peoples of the underdeveloped lands the confidence that the task can be done—that people can better their economic conditions.

Knowing what needs to be done in the matter of economic development and how it should be done is a very complex business. I sometimes think we pay too little attention in this connection to the lessons of our own national developmental experience. When we consult with another government over a problem of economic development, usually one of the first steps is the dispatch of some sort of economic survey mission to explore the resources of the country in question. This approach is fine, as far as it goes, and it is a necessary one if an intelligent program is to be formulated. But the survey approach doesn't go very far. It is the subsequent action that counts. There is danger that the governments of the underdeveloped areas will fall victim to the illusion that the survey itself is the end product, rather than the starting point.

No survey preceded the onward march of American economic progress. Indeed, no survey which might have been made 150 or 100 or even 50 years ago could have charted or foreseen all the steps that would afterwards need to be taken. The point I am emphasizing is that economic development is a dynamic process of change and adaptation to change. New circumstances create new problems. Solutions to those problems create new circumstances. New techniques are developed or applied and in consequence the old economic balance is disturbed and again new problems arise.

We have been through this dynamic process. We have learned by doing, and our collective knowledge is now embodied in our people—in our businessmen, our agricultural specialists, our medical experts, our labor leaders, our public administrators, our educators. Our knowledge—or rather much of it—cannot be written down in books. It is that intangible factor called "know-how." It is the ability based on past experiment and experience, to find the right step to take next. This is what we can extend to the underdeveloped areas of the world. By providing it, we will be providing leadership. Here is a challenge to us.

It is a challenge to the American Government to assist in those aspects of economic development that pertain properly to the functions of government. Taxation, agriculture, research, public health, general education, and sanitation are all related to economic progress, and are all primarily the responsibility of government. Some of the finance required for progress in these fields must come through government channels.

To an even greater extent, however, this is a challenge to the whole American people, and to the private enterprise system which has been responsible for our own economic progress. Most of the job of development cannot be done by governments, but only by private citizens and organizations. Government initiative can build roads and dams, but governments have shown no great capacity for building tire factories. The technology, entrepreneurial ability, and initiative available through private companies or consultants is infinitely greater and more flexible than that available to governments.

There is a challenge to American business, and to business and professional men, to make available to the world their techniques and skills, and, naturally, to make profits. Americans are not being called to a crusade of altruism. They are being challenged to show the stuff of which they are made, to show the underdeveloped areas of the world how vision and the restless quest for new opportunities can build up underdeveloped countries by the creation of new wealth, wealth which enhances both the developer and the developed.

If Americans will rise to this challenge, we cannot fail to make an enormous contribution to the economic advancement of the underdeveloped areas. We can introduce into those areas the driving force of private initiative and the broadening influence of free enterprise. We can release the energies of the peoples of these areas so that they can work effectively for the kind of life they desire. We know that our system has worked. It has produced here a free, peace-loving and prosperous nation. We know that it can be made to work elsewhere. To make it work in the under-developed areas is the challenge that confronts us. If we do not rise to that challenge, the mantle of world leadership will pass to another system and another people.

CHARLES P. ISSAWI

The Near Eastern Economy in the World, and Its Possibilities of Development

I believe it was the distinguished French sociologist, François Le Play, who said that in the Social Sciences there were two sources of error, statistics and downright lying. I am afraid that I cannot spare you the statistics.

For the purposes of this paper, the Near East will be defined as the quadrant-shaped region consisting of Turkey, Iran, and Afghanistan in the north, the Arabian peninsula and the Fertile Crescent in the center, and the Nile Valley in the south. Its area is about 10 million square kilometers, roughly the same as that of Europe. Its population is 100 million, or about 4 per cent of the world's population. Of these 100 million, a little under half are Arabic speaking.

What then is the economic, as distinct from the political, strategic, religious, and cultural importance of the region? At first sight one is tempted to say, very little. The total industrial population of the region, including craftsmen, does not, in spite of the increase of the last two decades, exceed two million, or about 1 per cent of the world total, and the percentage of world industrial production accounted for by the Near East is probably smaller since its industry is little mechanized, not only in comparison with that of North America, Western and Eastern Europe, and the Soviet Union, but even compared to that of Latin America and certain parts of Asia. Excluding oil, a very important exception, its proved mineral resources are very small, consisting mainly of coal, iron, copper, and chrome in Turkey, phosphate, manganese, and iron in Egypt, and potash in the Dead Sea. But it should be added that much of the region has not been surveyed, while the greater part has been very imperfectly studied. Hence, proved reserves may not constitute an accurate index of the Near East's mineral resources.

Turning to agriculture, the main branch of activity which absorbs some four-fifths of the population, it will be seen that the Near East accounts for about one-thirtieth of the world's grain acreage and for the same proportion of aggregate world production of the principal grains. The Near East does, however, play a much more important part in the production of some other crops, notably long staple cotton in Egypt and the Sudan, olives and oranges in Turkey, Syria, Lebanon, and Israel, tobacco in Turkey and Syria, and dates and other fruits in Iraq, Turkey, Iran, Syria, and Lebanon.

The commercial importance of the region is commensurate with that of its agricultural and industrial output. The Near East accounts for some 3 per cent of total world trade. Its exports consist almost entirely of mineral and agricultural products, while its imports cover a wide range of foodstuffs, fuels, capital equipment, and manufactured goods.

At this point the economist might be tempted to dismiss the region as a backwater, quite outside the main stream of world economic activity. Such a judgment would, however, be completely mistaken since it fails to take into account the region's two main assets: its location, and its oil reserves.

The location of the Near East has a unique economic, as well as strategic and political importance. It is not merely that it marks the point where three continents converge and that it guards the approaches to both the western sea, the Mediterranean, and the eastern sea, the Indian Ocean. It is that, as was pointed out by Arnold Toynbee,

in an air age the locus of the centre of gravity of human affairs may be determined not by physical but human geography: not by the layout of oceans and seas, steppes and deserts, rivers and mountain ranges, passes and straits, but by the distribution of human numbers, energy, ability, skill, and character. And, among these human factors, the weight of numbers may eventually come to count for more than its influence in the past.*

* *Civilization on Trial* (London, 1948), p. 92.

Now the Near East is situated exactly between the two largest population masses in the world, that of Europe and that of Southeast Asia. Nor does the matter end there, for the Near East stands halfway between the two largest undeveloped stretches of land in the old world, near what Mackinder called the Northern and Southern Heartlands, the plains of Siberia and the savannahs of Central Africa. No wonder then that, in addition to possessing the leading international waterway, the Suez Canal, the region has become a nodal point of international airlines. In 1948, in addition to the sixteen locally owned and operated airlines, there were fourteen foreign airlines, representing eleven nationalities, which stopped at one or more Near Eastern airports. Some of the Near Eastern airports, notably the newly opened one at Beirut, rank with the world's finest.

Finally there is oil, a subject on which books could be and have been written. Here, however, a few bare facts must suffice. The bulk of the world's oil reserves seems to lie in two areas, one in the western hemisphere, centered on the Caribbean Sea and one in the eastern hemisphere, centered south of the Caucasus. The latest estimate puts the world's proved reserves at 78 billion barrels. Of these, 33 billion, or 42 per cent, lie in the Near East; 35 per cent in the United States; 10 per cent in the Soviet Union, and most of the remainder in the Caribbean countries of Latin America. Moreover, the potential reserves of the Near East are believed to be much larger than its discovered reserves and it is likely that, in a few years' time, the area will account for more than half the proved reserves of the world. It should, incidentally, be pointed out that the bulk of the region's reserves are concentrated in the Persian Gulf area, the richest country being tiny Kuwait, with 11 billion barrels, followed by Iran, Saudi Arabia, Iraq, and Qatar. The other producers include Egypt, Bahrain and, recently, Turkey, and deposits are known to exist in Northern Iran and Afghanistan and probably in Syria and Yemen as well. Indeed, it is unlikely that any Near Eastern country is totally devoid of oil.

But it is not only a question of quantity. Near Eastern oil is not only present on a large scale but it is also readily available. For, in the first place, practically all of the oil of the area is extracted by free flow, whereas almost all the oil produced in other parts of the world is brought to the surface by artificial lift, a fact which considerably increases its costs of production. Moreover, the average productivity of Near Eastern oil wells is incomparably greater than that of other areas. In 1948, the average daily production per well in the three major producers, Iran, Saudi Arabia, and Kuwait, was almost 7000 barrels. During the same year, the world average was only 20 barrels and the United States average 13 barrels.* It is unnecessary to elaborate the point, since its economic significance is evident.

In addition, from the point of view of producers, Near Eastern oil enjoys several other advantages. For in the first place, labor costs are low. Wages paid to oil workers, though somewhat above the rate prevalent in other Near Eastern industries, are much below those paid in American or Venezuelan fields. Owing to the very favorable natural conditions and the excellent equipment used, the average production of Near Eastern workers in the oil industry seems to be only slightly below that of Venezuelan and American workers. It is clear that labor costs are quite exceptionally low in the Near East. Secondly, royalties and other duties paid to Near Eastern governments are relatively small, averaging in 1948 about one-third the amount paid to the Venezuelan Government.† Finally, transport costs from the Mediterranean coast to Western Europe, the chief market for Near Eastern oil, are distinctly below those from the Caribbean area, and a further reduction may be expected with the completion of the pipelines under construction. As a result of all this, Near Eastern oil has been consistently underselling Caribbean oil and capturing an increasing share of European markets.

In these circumstances, it is not surprising to find that both the absolute production of the region and its share in world produc-

* The discrepancy between the figures for the Near East and those for the United States is due partly to geological factors and partly to the nature of the concessions, which allow the oil companies to adopt the most efficient methods of production.

† In the last two years royalty rates have been substantially raised in most of the major producing countries, but the Near Eastern level is still well below that of Venezuela.

tion are increasing very rapidly. The latter more than doubled between 1944 and 1948, when it stood at 430 million barrels, or over one-eighth of the world total, and in 1949 it rose to 528 million barrels, or one-sixth of world production. But even at this higher rate, the Near East is drawing on its proved reserves at the rate of a little over 1½ per cent, compared to over 9 per cent in the United States. And, as was pointed out earlier, there is good reason to believe that potential reserves are considerably greater than proved reserves.

Oil, then, is by far the most important of the natural resources of the Near East. But by itself it is far from solving the economic problems of the area. For, in the first place, several of the largest and most populous countries of the area produce little or no oil—for example, Turkey, Afghanistan, Egypt, and the Sudan. Secondly, even in some countries whose oil production is considerable, such as Iran and Iraq, it is unlikely that the total local expenditures of the oil companies, both in the form of royalties and other payments to governments and in the form of wages, represent an addition of more than 10 per cent to the national income. And, unlike manufacturing industries, oil does not produce much secondary employment and income. (This, of course, is not to deny that these expenditures constitute a substantial proportion of the governments' budgets and the countries' receipts of foreign exchange.) Lastly, although Near Eastern oil reserves are large they are not inexhaustible. Hence receipts accruing from them should be regarded as drawings on capital and should be used to build up productive power so as to provide alternative sources of employment and income. Up to now this has been done only to a quite limited extent.

Indeed such a development of resources is imperative over all the region if the already very low standard of living is to be maintained, let alone raised. During the past ten or fifteen years there has been some noteworthy progress in industry, agriculture, and transport, but in general this has failed to keep pace with the growth of the population, which is increasing at a yearly rate of between 1 and 1½ per cent. In some countries there is distinct evidence of a decline in the standard of living.

In all the Near Eastern countries there is some land, and in some there are huge tracts, which could be brought under cultivation through irrigation or mechanization or a combination of both. In all, agricultural methods leave much to be desired and great improvements could be introduced in plants and livestock, tools, sowing practices, storage and preservation facillties, and so on. In all countries, though in varying degrees, means of transport stand in need of extension and improvement. Finally, in all, industry must be expanded severalfold, and this can be achieved, in spite of such obstacles as the paucity of raw materials and the lack of skilled workers and technicians, provided industrial expansion is integrated with a development of agriculture which will provide it with raw materials and a market for its goods.

The essential pre-conditions of such a development are three. There must be, first, a vigorous drive to raise the educational, social, and hygienic level of the masses. There must, secondly, be an economic integration between the different countries of the area, since each by itself is far too small to provide a market for modern industries. Of course, in some cases political divergences make such a union impossible, but over most of the area there are no such obstacles. Finally, there must be an enormous capital investment, which should be measured in hundreds of millions of dollars and which would bring with it the necessary technical skills, which are essential.

This last point requires elaboration. The investment must be large enough not only to bring about an expansion in a few directions, but to achieve an integrated all-round development in a relatively short time. The development must be integrated; agriculture, industry, and transport must advance simultaneously, each helping the others. Otherwise, each will merely come to a dead end and find that it produces "more than the market can absorb." And the development must be rapid enough to outstrip the population growth and bring about a rise in the standard of living, for such a rise alone can set in motion forces which can check that growth. Otherwise, the increased production will merely serve to support a larger and ever-increasing population.

At present, the Near Eastern countries are caught in a vicious circle. Their low income drastically limits their power to save and invest, and their low investment prevents them from raising their income. There are only two ways of breaking this circle.

The first is for foreign capital to enter the field in force, in alliance with local capital. Since normal commercial incentives may not prove powerful enough to attract sufficient amounts of capital, much reliance will have to be placed on such institutions as the International Bank for Reconstruction and Development and the Export-Import Bank. The partnership of foreign and local capital is in every respect ideal since the presence of local capital serves as an attraction for foreign capital while the entry of foreign capital would stimulate local saving and investment.

Failing such foreign investment, only one possibility remains open to the Near Eastern countries: to provide investment funds from their own savings. This would require a reduction of consumption below its already depressed level and a mobilization of savings by the imposition of severe government controls. Mohammed Ali's attempt, more than a hundred years ago, as well as that of Turkey in the 1930's, shows that such a method is possible; it would be, however, not only painful but highly wasteful. For it would mean that the Near Eastern countries would be denied that foreign help without which industrialization has never taken place, except in eighteenth-century England. And this at a time when the United States, and to a lesser extent Britain, have large amounts of capital which could be employed more profitably abroad than at home. Only the lack of coöperation of this country and Britain could justify the Near East in striving to finance its industrialization from its own resources.

It remains to add, however, that as long as the present international tension continues it is unlikely that much foreign capital will be forthcoming. Even the industries already established in the area are showing caution. Thus the decision to build the refineries processing Near Eastern oil not in the area but in the Western European markets may be justified on political and military grounds, but certainly not on economic. This merely illustrates once more the fact that today all parts of the world are indissolubly intertwined and that no single country or region, and certainly not one as centrally located as the Near East, can hope to work out its salvation in a world at war with itself.

(The author is a member of the Secretariat of the United Nations, but the views expressed in this article are purely personal and do not necessarily reflect the opinions of the United Nations or any other organization.)

LEONID I. STRAKHOVSKY

The Nature of Soviet Propaganda in the Near East

The position of the Soviet Union in the Near East is intrinsically very different from the position of Russia as we know it historically. A seeming truism, but never too old to be repeated, appeared recently in an article by our eminent socialist, Norman Thomas, on the question of our ideological fight with communism. He would be understood by almost any intelligent person devoid of bias:

> It would be completely accurate [he said] to say that communist ethics are frankly based on the key principle: that is right which helps communism to power and maintains it in power; that is wrong which hinders it; and the leaders of the communist movement are the sole judges of the application of this principle.*

Once we admit that this is the attitude of the leaders of the Soviet Union today, then it will be easier to understand why there are so many contradictions in the application of this policy all over the world and particularly in the Near East, because in the Near East, besides Moslem Arabs and the Jewish citizens of Israel, there are many Christians of different denominations. We find that the Soviet Union applies one set of tactics toward the Arabs, another set toward the Jews, and an entirely different set toward the Christians.

Toward the Arabs the Russians have tried from the beginning to appear as protectors of their spirit of independence, and they try to inculcate in the younger generation the ideas of dialectical materialism and to lead them away from their old Moslem religion.

With the Jews the problem has been somewhat different. When the state of Israel came into being there was such great enthusiasm

* *New York Times,* August 6, 1950.

among the mass of seven million Jews within the confines of the Soviet Union and its satellites that the Soviet government became alarmed. Many Jews in the Soviet Union attempted to emigrate from the Soviet Union to Israel, but no one is permitted to emigrate from the Soviet Union, neither Jew nor Gentile, and it fell upon the Soviet government to entrust one of its foremost Jewish writers, Ilya Ehrenburg, to insult openly the ambassadress of the state of Israel to the Soviet Union, a Jewish lady who was born in Russia. When at a reception in the Embassy, she addressed Ilya Ehrenburg in English (since the ambassadress had lived most of her life in the United States), Ilya Ehrenburg verbally slapped her by saying, "I hate any Russian Jew who addresses me in English."

It is evident that the Soviet Union does not want its Jewish population to leave, as it does not want any of its subjects to leave, because whoever escapes its clutches is a potential anti-Soviet propagandist.

In the case of the Christian population of the Near East, the Soviet Union employs different tactics. The leaders of the Kremlin have never underestimated the power of religion; hence they fought religion from the moment they came to power in 1917. During the last war they realized that a vast group of Soviet citizens were still devotedly attached to their religion, the Russian Orthodox faith. Over night the policy of the Soviet Union toward the organized Russian Orthodox Church changed. The Church was recognized as an agent of the government; the patriarchate was reëstablished; and the Church was permitted for the first time since the Revolution to have seminaries in which to train future priests. In Palestine, beyond the confines of the Soviet Union, was a very important nucleus of Russian Orthodox interest, most of it in the state of Israel. From the end of the eighteenth century, the Russian Orthodox people and the Imperial Russian government had invested great amounts of money in real estate, churches, monasteries, hostelries, and other properties not only in Jerusalem but in other parts of Palestine, since Palestine, the Holy Land, was the goal of all great pilgrimages of the devout Russians. After the revolution of 1917, the administration of those vast possessions was under a council of bishops which broke away from the Moscow church because that church was completely subject to communist rule, and for thirty years this council of bishops cared for the property in Palestine. But by the end of 1948, the Soviet Union, in agreement with the government of Israel, obtained possession of these properties. The old council of bishops was politely shown out and a spiritual mission of the Russian Orthodox Church to the Holy Land, headed by Abbot Leonid (Lobachyov) of the Moscow episcopate was recognized as its successor. Abbot Leonid, appointed by the patriarch Alexis, left Moscow with his retinue on November 23, 1948. Upon his arrival, the mission took over the old missions and the various religious buildings in Jerusalem, the Church of SS. Peter and Paul in Jaffa, the Church of St. Elias on Mount Carmel, and a convent at Ain Karem with fifty-eight Russian nuns.* This was only the beginning, because, as has been said, the property of the Russian Orthodox Church in Palestine is very extensive. Since then, gradually most of that property has come under the jurisdiction of the spiritual mission of the Russian Orthodox Church in Palestine.

All this may appear to be insignificant, yet it is very important, because the members of the hierarchy of the Russian Orthodox Church are propagandists for the power of the Soviet Union. They are not propagandists of communism, of course, but they go about saying that the Soviet state and the Russian Orthodox Church live peaceably together. In their support of the Soviet rulers they rely on the answer Christ gave to one of his questioners, who had asked whether he should pay his taxes in the coin that bore the effigy of Caesar, "Render therefore unto Caesar the things which are Caesar's; and unto God the things that are God's." So these ecclesiastics go about saying that a Russian Orthodox person can be a good Russian Orthodox and yet be a citizen of the Soviet Union, and ever since the establishment of the spiritual mission of the Russian Orthodox Church of the Patriarchate of Moscow in Jerusalem, with jurisdiction over parts of the Holy Land as well, this has become the continuous line of propaganda in favor of the Soviet Union among many of the younger generation of the Christians in the Near East. That the Russian Orthodox Church is being used

* *Edinaya Tserkov,* 3, nos. 7–8 (1949), 20.

by the Soviet government for its own end is furthermore substantiated by the fact that representatives of that Church attended all so-called peace conferences sponsored by Communists and leftists, with the exception of the one held in New York. Thus, the conference held in Paris in April 1949 was attended by a Bishop Nicholas of the Archdiocese of Moscow with a retinue of ecclesiastics forming part of the Soviet delegation; the same was true in Stockholm where the famous Peace Congress was held—and during its sequel held in Moscow.

You may ask, "How is all this possible?" And the answer may be found in that truism that all means are good for a Communist as long as they help achieve the desired aim. The Communists' professed aim in the Near East, as Mr. Hall pointed out, is to create a stable and friendly state of affairs. Stable from their own point of view, friendly also from their own point of view. This could be achieved only through a social revolution and so whether by the use of religion or of force, the Soviet Union is endeavoring to bring about a state of affairs in the Near East which will be favorable to Moscow. In a recent issue of the magazine *New Time,** which is one of the main mouthpieces of Soviet propaganda and is published not only in Russian, but also in English, French, German, and Polish, an article appeared commenting on the declaration of the three Western foreign ministers in London on May 25, a declaration concerning the Near East. It starts with abusive language, which I would not dare to translate—since Soviet publications use language which we would consider unprintable. Then it states that the real aims of that declaration actually smack of another venture in Anglo-American military imperialism and are a part of "total diplomacy," though ostensibly the declaration purports to guarantee the present frontiers of the Near Eastern states and offers to supply arms and military equipment to the Arab countries and to the state of Israel for the purpose of guaranteeing their internal safety and legitimate defense, as well as enabling them to play their part in the general defense of the region. Then the article proceeds to say that

* Yu. Zvyagin, "Total Diplomacy in the Near East," *New Time,* 27 (269), July 5, 1950, 11.

the publication of this document, which by its content and especially by its clumsy phraseology reminds one of the text of the North Atlantic Pact, leaves no doubt that from now on the Near East also is to be found in the very center of the renowned total diplomacy . . . The public-spirited groups of the Near Eastern countries responded to the publication of this triple declaration with an outburst of indignation. The appearance of this document is an act of rude intervention on the part of the imperialists in the internal affairs of Near Eastern states with the purpose of unceremonious exploitation of the latter for the benefit of their own militaristic and adventurous plans. The Tripartite declaration is a menace to the life interests and to the very independence of the peoples of the Near East. Before them stands the task of solidifying the democratic forces and of uniting the efforts of all honest patriots in their struggle for the independence of their countries and for peace and democracy.

The Soviets play not only on the secular minds of the younger Moslem generation, not only on the religious mind of the Christians in the Near East; they play also on the nationalism which is found in every state of the Near East today. And they will play on all these human emotions to the best of their ability if they are not stopped by a rational approach to the Near East which has nothing to do with economics, with oil wells, or with the well-being of people; it has to do with the expression of complete self-interest. The people of the Near East will survive only if they realize that they must make a choice now between East and West. And if they do not choose the West, they will succumb to the East, and the East means the Soviet Union, totalitarianism and concentration camps.

Conclusion

I must emphasize that I am strictly an amateur and neophyte on the subject of the Near East. I went out there entirely as a sort of American innocent abroad and came back simply as an American who had to undergo a very thorough process of "acculturation." My stay in the Near East was a series of incidents like the following two. A day or two after I arrived in Jerusalem in June 1947, I was invited to the home of a rabbi for dinner. It was my first time in the home of a rabbi, and that on a Friday evening. This person happened to be a rabbi who had an Irish sense of humor. Fortunately for me indeed, he had been for a number of years the chief rabbi in Ireland. As I walked into his home, I was handed the small black cap known as the "yomelka." It was the first time that I had come into possession of this kind of cap and it developed that I had not been fitted for size. I was told to put the yomelka on my head which I did quite dutifully. Subsequently we went into dinner and the soup course was set before us. Before we began to eat, the rabbi said some words in Hebrew which were unknown to me, but it was clear that they called for some gesture of devotion. So rather subconsciously I bowed my head with results that must be apparent. I began my work in Palestine by "dunking a yomelka," in the home of the chief rabbi. It took me some time to live that down.

Subsequently, in our armistice negotiation at Rhodes, a member of the Arab delegations came to me one day and said that we were not making any progress on the negotiations. He suggested that I call an adjournment to the meetings and send the delegations home, and perhaps at some later date they could come back and find a basis for agreement. "Rhodes is not an exciting place," he said, "so we might as well go home." I told him that as a representative of the United Nations I would not send them home. In a sense the delegations there were trapped because once having brought them to the island the negotiations would continue until one or both of the delegations themselves would take the responsibility for breaking them off. Then I became bold, or what I thought was bold, although not at all in a Near Eastern sense. For I said in a threatening manner, "I am prepared to sit here until you reach agreement." "In fact," I said, boasting, "I am prepared to sit for ten years on this island waiting for you to reach agreement." Then I sat back looking for the shock. The Arab representative looked at me somewhat puzzled and a little blandly, and quietly said, *"Only* ten years, what's your hurry?" I came to appreciate fully just what the time factor means in the Near East.

It seems to me that perhaps the most significant problem to emerge from the various papers—the most vital facet of the entire subject of our relations with the Near East—is one which we have touched upon only lightly, if at all. That problem, as I see it, is how to reach and make a constructive, lasting, sympathetic impact upon the peoples of an area such as the Near East, and moreover with a purpose in view in making that impact. We have just seen in the paper of Dr. Malik that the West after long years, indeed despite long years of close contact with the Near East and its peoples, has not won either their admiration or their confidence. The Near East is an area, and I hasten to point out that it is by no means a unique area—other such areas are the Far East, Southeast Asia, Africa, and the Caribbean—in which poverty, human misery, and economic underdevelopment are so widespread as to be generally characteristic. At the same time the peoples of the Near East, having an ancient history, are proud, sensitive, resentful of outside interference, and justifiably suspicious of the motives of the outside influences presently at work in their area. Now, in general terms, the broad aims in the Near East of the Western powers—especially of our own government and of the government of the United Kingdom—are defined within the general framework of economic and social well-being, free governments, free institutions, and fundamental human rights. Despite this fact, it is also

71

true that the specific expressions of the broad policies of these governments, whether they may be political or economic, often, if not always, tend to reflect the national self-interests of the great powers. At least it is what may be interpreted by them to represent their immediate essential national self-interests relative to the people of the Near East. If that is so, then the crucial question certainly is—To what extent do the national self-interest policies of great powers conflict with the ultimate basic interests, aspirations, and well-being of the peoples of the Near East? On the basis of past experience, it would appear that there is often a clash in this regard.

As we define it, the basic issue in the world today is freedom, freedom in our sense—in the Western sense. Free peoples, free governments, to put it in another way, are engaged in a struggle between democracy and communism, and this being so, it is to our vital interest to reach the peoples of underdeveloped areas, to reach them with a more effective appeal than the appeal of communism. In this sense economic assistance to such peoples is an indispensable investment for us. It is not a humanitarian enterprise; it is in the long range a self-interested investment. And this obviously is an investment which cannot be undertaken on a bargain-basement basis. So the question is whether by a very generous policy of economic assistance, and I mean by very generous something much broader in scope than anything that we have contemplated up to now, we could in fact do much to minimize future possibilities of far more costly military operations such as that in which we now unfortunately find ourselves engaged in Korea. Finally we must always put to ourselves the question—What now are we offering the peoples of the Near East? We must help them to help themselves and give assurance of our good will and our hope that they can with such assistance find a way out of the poverty in which they find themselves. We must give them assurances that we believe in applied freedom and democracy.

I would not wish to conclude without saying, from my own experience in connection with the Palestine question, that I am concerned about what appears to be a tendency among the Western states toward a policy of drift with regard to the Near East. This perhaps was an unfortunate by-product of the armistice agreements, which tended to remove some of the sense of urgency which had impelled the Western states in the United Nations to exert great efforts toward a settlement of the Palestine question. The immediate sense of urgency has been dulled by the existence of the armistice agreements. But I think it is important to warn that the Near East remains a problem area, and from the standpoint of our interests in a global sense, is most certainly a dangerous spot. It will remain a dangerous spot until much more progress toward a peaceful settlement of the differences between the Arab states and Israel has been made than is the case today. I feel that the main obstacle to moving beyond the uneasy armistice stage which now prevails is the Arab refugee problem. I do not in any sense feel that it is an insoluble problem, but I feel that it will take some effort of a much more concentrated nature than has been attempted during the past year by the United Nations.

MORTIMER GRAVES

A Cultural Relations Policy in the Near East

The question of a cultural relations policy for the United States in the Near East is easily dismissed; a cultural relations policy between any two civilizations is simply that each should know as much as possible about the other. This policy is undoubtedly completely acceptable, and consequently, it is not so much the policy as the steps which must be taken to bring the policy to fruition—that is to say, the cultural relations *program* between the United States and the Near East—which I wish to discuss.

In our frame of reference presumably a cultural relations program means a program of government. In those prewar days which we now probably too optimistically call normal we did, indeed, have cultural relations at least with Western European nations, but we did not need cultural relations programs. The scholars of Western Europe knew the scholars of the United States personally; their respective publications circulated easily in the normal commercial channels of trade; everybody read everybody else's language; a scholarly brawl could be easily made to encompass the whole scholarly world.

This happy state of affairs has never existed in our cultural relations with the Near East. Censorship, regulation, and man-made barriers to international intercourse have always had a higher inci-

74

dence in the Near East than with us. The commercial interchange of publications and other results of study and research has been subject to all the handicaps of other commercial exchange between East and West, principally, of course, the vast difference in monetary power. And finally there was this formidable wall of the languages which few Americans knew. In our postwar cultural relations with Europe, consequently, we need speak only of reëstablishing bonds which have been temporarily disrupted; with respect to the Near East, on the other hand, we have to create something new, something which has never existed, at least in the experience of living men or their grandfathers. It is this difference which makes the intervention of government and discussion in terms of program necessary.

The first element in our cultural relations program with the Near East must be that more, many more, Americans must know much more about the Near East. This means the development within our academic structure of more scientific concern with the area and its peoples—especially at the level of what goes on in their minds. I must insist on this last element—knowledge of what the Near East thinks and aspires to. Our very materialistic culture which prides itself on its so-called practicality finds itself too easily satisfied with a knowledge of the economics, the political and social structure, the human ecology, of those cultures which it tries to understand. It must always be remembered that, in the Near East as in so many of the regions which we in our overweening pride call "backward," the major problem is intellectual, that of accommodating ancient modes of thought to life in the world of the twentieth century. Unless we can understand the Near East at this level all our programs of assistance to the Near East will be in vain. There is not the slightest use in our helping the Near East to increase its productive capacity unless at the same time it can make progress towards the settlement of its intellectual, cultural, political, and social problems.

This better American knowledge and understanding of the cultures of the Near East we might earlier have left to our academic structure, our colleges and universities, our libraries and museums.

Unfortunately our academic structure is not prepared to accept this burden. I do not need to cite elaborate examples; just take the best university you happen to think of—whichever one it may be—and reflect the pattern of its offerings against any pattern that represents the totality of significant cultures of the world with which we—in the position of world leadership which we are somewhat reluctantly assuming—have to deal. You will discover that the academic structure is almost as West European centered as it was when Mecca was practically as far away as the moon.

This reorientation of our academic structure away from its West European centeredness into something like a world-perspective is one of the most formidable tasks of our day. It is quite true that the past quarter century has seen not a little progress in this direction, especially with respect to the Far East and Russia, much less with respect to the area of our present concern. But with the best will in the world on the part of academic administrations the problem is just too difficult for any of them to make much progress. I have become convinced that this reorientation can take place only with the expenditure of large social capital, and that, in our political structure, means Federal Government funds. Even the large foundations, generous as they have been in this direction, can do little but the experimental work; they can provide the venture capital with which we take the chances which will tell us what is to be done when the real money is available, but they cannot do the job, certainly not at the tempo at which it has to be done.

This phase of our problem, then, resolves itself into discussion of what the Federal Government might appropriately do. Without going deeply into this question here, I can point out two or three directions in which the government might proceed without involving any radical departure from functions which are already considered completely germane to it. In the first place, the Library of Congress might have as its goal the possession and servicing—much more important and expensive—of every significant publication in every important Near Eastern language published since 1900. Doubtless this is an impossible goal, but it is one which our Congress ought to recognize as a measure of our national security.

second, I see no reason why there should not be government fellowships in Near Eastern studies precisely as there are government fellowships in atomic science. The one is just as important to the national security as the other. Third, government could contract with universities and other non-profit organizations for the production of the tools of study and research which we do not have for the Near East, just as it did for the production of language and area manuals during our most recent war.

One other way in which government might participate in the development of better American understanding of the Near East demands, perhaps, a little longer explanation. In our commercial relations with all countries of the Near East we have the phenomenon which is known as the dollar gap, that is to say they buy from us more goods than they can pay for in dollars. For some reason which nobody can fathom, this is called a favorable balance of trade; its result is that we have in every Near Eastern country a reservoir of indigenous currency which cannot be converted into dollars except at fantastic loss unless we can discover something in those countries which we are willing to accept as imports. I propose that we commence importing cultural goods and services. We might begin with books; there is no satisfactory library of books and other printed materials from any Near Eastern country in the United States; we need a dozen of them. Some of these books, periodicals, and so forth, are so significant for understanding what is going on in the Near Eastern mind that they should be translated into English; let us have them translated with this uncollectible currency. Near Eastern countries contain monuments of our culture which they cannot maintain and repair, they have manuscripts and objects of art which we want to study but which they cannot afford to catalogue and make available. What a contribution we could make to world scholarship, and incidentally to understanding, by accepting these services which we need in partial extinguishment of dollars which we can never collect! Finally, for our own purposes the indigenous academic structure of the Near East must be strengthened; until there are the facilities in Near Eastern universities for adequate study of Near Eastern phenomena, in economics, political science, over the whole realm of the humanities and the social sciences, *our* study of the cultures of the region will be handicapped. No American contribution to Near Eastern Welfare could be so great as that which could be made by a major American effort to help the Near East build an upper academic structure consonant with twentieth-century needs. It is almost pathetic to realize that this could be done in large part with indigenous currencies representing dollars that we shall never be able to collect.

Moreover, any intelligent cultural relations program between the United States and the Near East must involve much better American understanding of the forces which are contending with the American idea for acceptance by the Near East. The principal of these are, of course, communism and Islam. Americans who understand neither are at a terrible handicap when they try to explain what the American way has to offer in competition. For it must be remembered that in the struggle for the minds of these non-West European peoples both Marxist and Moslem thought make the appeal that they provide a better accommodation of ancient ways of thinking to life in the twentieth century than does that anarchic, anachronous, amorphous thing which we call our democracy and which happens to suit our historical experience and tradition. We can evaluate our society by its material product and find it good, but it may be that other societies want it evaluated in different terms, as a total way of life. Here we speak with less assurance for few Americans have tried to explain America; I might say that few Americans understand America in terms acceptable to societies with different cultural experiences and historical traditions.

In short, a cultural relations program with the Near East must involve three departures new for Americans: many more Americans with fundamental knowledge of the Near East, especially at the level of Near Eastern thought and aspiration; more nearly a world-centered academic structure; and much better understanding of the American picture itself. Without these, the export of American capital and American "know-how" in an effort to increase the productive power of the Near East without contribution oward the settlement *pari passu* of the Near East's intellectual, cultural, social, political problems, will do more harm than good.*

* Francis O. Wilcox, Chief of Staff of the Senate Foreign Relations Committee, remarked: "In connection with the problem of developing an informed public opinion, we who work for the Legislative Branch are particularly anxious to do what we can to build in the Congress a better understanding of what is going on in the various areas of the world. There are at least two very effective ways of doing that. When a crisis develops in our relations with a particular area or country, as in the case of China and Palestine, then you have a great deal of interest evidenced on the part of Members of the Congress. Similarly, when the Administration presents us with an important treaty or legislative measure like the North Atlantic Treaty or the European Recovery Program, a considerable amount of interest is created.

"If one looks over the legislative program since the war, however, he will find that Congress has had before it a good many important problems relating to various parts of the world, but very few relating to the Near East. We have had the United Nations Charter, the Rio Treaty, the Military Assistance Program, the North Atlantic Treaty, the European Recovery Program, aid for China and Korea, and a good many other matters relating to the United Nations particularly. We have had, I think, only one or two rather specific programs in the Near Eastern field, such as extension of aid to Palestine refugees and our program of assistance to Greece and Turkey.

"As a result, the Near East is one of the important areas of the world which has been neglected in congressional thinking, and how to stimulate interest in the Congress with respect to this area is a difficult problem. Of course, we are confronted with somewhat the same dilemma in stimulating interest in the American public generally, but my immediate concern is the Congress. Obviously, we can't go around stirring up crises in the world, and it is unwise to sit back and wait for legislation before a basic foundation of information is laid.

"An incomplete answer to this problem might lie in the subcommittee system which has been created by the House Committee on Foreign Affairs and the Senate Committee on Foreign Relations. On the Senate side we have a subcommittee of three members who are available for consultation from time to time with top officials in the Department of State on Near and Middle Eastern questions. I am hopeful that this device will do much to keep the Foreign Relations Committee currently informed with respect to major developments in that area and will help make the members of the Committee aware of the real significance of the Near East in American foreign policy. This procedure, of course, will not meet the issue with respect to the Congress generally."

GEORGE CAMP KEISER

The Middle East Institute: Its Inception and Its Place in American International Studies

Shortly after the close of World War II, a small number of people in this country who had, for one reason or another, been interested in the world area south and east of the Mediterranean and west of what we call the Far East, became convinced that the lands having Islam for a common denominator should be better known to the Western world. Some had had an intimate association with the area as missionaries, others had known it through archaeology, still others—rather more romantically—as travelers. Previous to this time, these groups were small and tended to enjoy their interests as members of cultural circles rather than as groups launching forth in an effort to interest people of this country, generally, in a corner of the world known in the United States only to them.

At this time, however, there was an urgent reason why Americans should broaden their international understanding and, particularly, why concentration of their attention should be centered on the Near or—as it was coming to be known more and more—Middle East. It was in this particular area that we made our important connections with our then ally, Russia, and many of us were aware of the importance of the Middle East Command. In this area, also, the petroleum reservoirs bid fair not only to attract large capital investments from the West, but also to furnish oil to Europe and Asia in such vast quantities that the Middle East could not afford to be overlooked in the world of economics. For the United States, it meant the conservation of vast sources of this commodity in the Western Hemisphere, for our own purposes. Politically, the area was of increasing significance because of the

United Nations, in which the United States was becoming one of the most prominent members. Consequently, there seemed to be strong reasons why Americans should know more about the modern Middle East, but there appeared to be no organization set up to disseminate information concerning it. It was this urge that led to the founding of The Middle East Institute, in Washington, D. C., in May 1946.

During the past four years, there has been a growing interest in the Middle East on the part of Americans, but their knowledge of the area still leaves much to be desired. Before proceeding to take up some of the functions of the Institute, let me cite a few examples of our lack of understanding of this part of the world.

The first example is from a letter written by T. Cuyler Young, on August 4, 1950, to *The New York Times,* and cites "the linking of Iran with those other spots on the Soviet periphery where the Kremlin may be expected to strike through satellites in a war of attrition or of limited engagements." It went on to mention the erroneousness of the inclusion of Iran with Korea, Indo-China, Formosa, and Yugoslavia, asking the question, "Where is the satellite to do this in Iran?" A glance at the atlas will, of course, clarify the fact that Iran borders directly on the U.S.S.R. proper—there are *no* intervening satellites.

The second instance—a more general statement—taken from the same source, was a dispatch from New Delhi in which Prime Minister Nehru castigated the Western Powers for having adopted "decisions affecting vast areas of Asia, without understanding the real needs and mind of the people."

A third example stems from an entirely different source— namely, one having to do with Islamic architecture. Many of us are familiar with the delicate arcades of such buildings as the Alhambra, but some criticize the lacelike quality of its arches because they appear to be structurally unsound. Apparently these critics have not learned of the theory that such arches were not designed to carry superimposed weight, but that the arcades were built on a post and lintel principle, with the arches hung, like curtains, in the upper portions of the openings.

It seems unreasonable, therefore, to draw conclusions before understanding fundamental facts. These examples clearly show the lack of general knowledge of the Middle Eastern area prevalent among Americans today.

Let me now list some of the matters about which we should be better informed: knowledge of the philosophy of Islam; the importance of the Koranic law in directing the lives of the people in Moslem countries; the importance of the pilgrimage to Mecca in tying together the Moslem world; questions arising from increasing populations, including the necessity for improvement of public health; the rapid changes being brought about by air travel, television, and Western scientific development, generally.

But to sum up, all this is a new field for Americans, most of whom have had little occasion to think of it other than in terms of Ali Baba and Aladdin. Whether we like it or not, however, the lamp has been rubbed and filled with oil. Arabia is, in truth, a land of untold riches, and the magic carpet is at hand to carry us there by air in less time than it takes to travel from New York to San Francisco by the fastest train. The Middle East is our concern. We must find ways to become more familiar with it.

The Middle East Institute, it should be emphasized, is especially concerned with the present-day aspects of the area in question, and its function is primarily directed toward the education of Americans. It differs from most other organizations of learning, however, in that emphasis is placed upon the *modern* Middle East, and opportunity for general adult participation in its curriculum is stressed.

The Institute has expanded its activities in no small degree during the past four and one-half years it has been in operation. These activities fall, roughly, into four categories—publications, education, research, and information.

In the field of publication, *The Middle East Journal* was brought out in January 1947. Subsequently, there was added the *Newsletter,* which is issued to members of the organization at frequent intervals during the year. In the summer of 1950, a pamphlet entitled *Americans and the Middle East: Partners in the Next Decade* was issued, containing addresses and panel discussions from the Fourth Annual Conference of the Institute, held in

March 1950. Other publications of a similar nature are contemplated.

Middle East studies conducted under the auspices of the Institute fall into two categories: accredited courses on the graduate level, held at the School of Advanced International Studies of Johns Hopkins University, and at other institutions emphasizing work in this area; and lectures open to Institute members and their guests. Special language classes have been conducted by the Institute for its members, but such arrangements are dependent upon demand from year to year. Also in the nature of general education and information are the Institute conferences. So far, these have been limited to annual gatherings, but it is contemplated that, from time to time, meetings of this nature will be held as events may warrant special discussions of timely subjects concerning the area.

Research programs are another form of activity undertaken by the Institute. A recently formed committee on Islamic and modern, Near and Middle Eastern law, is at present collecting manuscripts from authorities on the subject, in contemplation of publishing a guide to the study of law in this area. Another program under way is that concerned with research in the social sciences in general.

A broad information program is in process of development. So far, only a few component parts of it have been set up, such as an extensive catalogue of names of individuals and organizations having significant Middle Eastern interests, compiled from a survey representing exhaustive research. Such a catalogue entails, however, an adequate staff to keep its information up to date by making current contacts with agencies through which new data are available. This service should, eventually, include information on important visitors to the United States, lectures on the area to be held throughout the country, arrangements for study here and abroad—including fellowship grants, introductions among people pursuing similar Middle Eastern activities, exchange of information on costs of living and travel in the area, and many other matters leading to a better mutual understanding between Americans and the people of the Middle East.

Naturally, no organization such as The Middle East Institute can go forward without problems which sometimes seem insurmountable. Opinions differ as to the implementation of ideas and the carrying out of programs.

There are indications, however, that its work has not been sufficiently publicized, and that it should make itself known to many who, apparently, are not yet aware of its existence. It is certainly the aim of the Middle East Institute to coöperate with as many other interested groups as possible, in order to carry on work on a wider and more useful scale.

H. A. R. GIBB

Oriental Studies in the United Kingdom

The recent developments in Oriental studies in England may seem paradoxical, when one remembers how for more than twenty years, when we were asked about the progress of Oriental studies in England, we had to admit, particularly just before the last war, that they were not going very well. When people from other countries said, "But you have all these commitments in the Near East and India and so on; surely you must have to train people for these services?" we could only reply, "Perhaps people are being trained, but they are not being trained at the universities." Now, since the war, there has come this extraordinary effort to build up a group of studies covering all the Asiatic, Slavonic, and African fields, and spread over the universities of England and Scotland, when the obvious need for government officials and technicians in the eastern countries, particularly India, is no longer at anything like its former level.

The Committee which drew up the Report that led to this new development, the Scarbrough Commission, was composed almost wholly of civil servants and former officials in the East, with very few academic representatives, none of them Orientalists. It was a surprise to us at the universities that the Commission came out with a decided demand for extensive subsidies from public funds for the development of Oriental, Slavonic, and African studies in a number of universities in England and Scotland.

The reason for this expansion, as one can see, is not the need for producing technicians or for training personnel to occupy official positions in the East. What lies behind it is the realization that the whole situation of the Western countries in regard to the countries of Asia and Africa has changed. We can no longer rely on that factor of prestige which seemed to play such a large part i prewar thinking, neither can we any longer expect the peoples c Asia and Africa or of Eastern Europe to come to us and lear from us, while we sit back. We have to learn about them so tha we can learn to work with them in a relationship that is closer t terms of mutuality. For that reason, something had to be done t build up a strong body of Oriental studies in England.

We were well off in the sense that we had a foundation on whic to build. There has been a tradition of Oriental studies in Englan for many centuries, but it has not always been a very active tradi tion, and has existed rather on the margins of academic life. W have been aiming to make that tradition more alive, to mak Oriental studies more central to the whole object of academi training, which is not technical training, but training for life. With out entering here on a discussion of the aims and purposes of uni versities, I can say that what we are trying to do is to set the stud of Oriental cultures and civilizations on a level with every kin of cultural study in the universities, as a study in its own right which carries with it a sound intellectual and cultural training and has the further advantage that it enables those who have gon through that training to understand and interpret to our own peopl the civilizations which they have been studying, and to meet thei peoples on an equal footing, not simply as officials and technicians It may be that some of our students will become officials, and per haps some of them will become technicians; but that is not the basic function of the whole development.

The breadth of the Scarbrough Commission's recommendations as mentioned before, came as something of a surprise to academic circles, and we hardly dared to hope that they would be put intc effect. But they were—both by the allocation of a considerable sum of money to be distributed to the universities through the Univer sity Grants Committee (the channel through which all public funds are distributed to universities in England), and by setting up an academic committee to advise the Treasury on the award of stu dentships to students who had proved themselves to be of first-class caliber.

We are at present not quite through the first half of the program.

So far as the development has gone, it has yielded good results. If the second half of the program is carried out (and that, I suppose, depends on circumstances which are not within anybody's control at the present moment), there is no doubt whatever that a very great step will have been taken to establish a basis on which, for the first time for many centuries, western scholars and a trained body of educated men and women in the West, not necessarily academic scholars, will meet the East on a plane of mutuality.

I do wish to emphasize that point, which I think comes very clearly in the papers of Mr. Graves and Mr. Hall, that the whole problem of a cultural program is to establish mutuality. Mutuality does not mean necessarily that you and the other man completely agree on each and every subject. It means that you understand, sympathize with, and comprehend the other man's problems and attitudes from the inside, and that he understands your problems and attitudes from the inside also. Now there was a time, down to somewhere near the end of the nineteenth century, when that kind of relationship seemed to be gradually growing up. There was, quite definitely in England and on the continent of Europe, an increasing awareness of and interest in and effort at understanding of Oriental cultures. Likewise in China and Japan, India, Turkey, and other countries of the Near East, there was a growing awareness of and understanding of Western culture.

Then something happened. Not only did we, in the Western countries, drop our interest and turn suddenly to other things, but in the Oriental countries also there was a similar reaction. On both sides there was less and less effort to reach out and achieve that attitude which I am calling mutuality. And, while sincerely agreeing, as I do, with what previous papers have expressed, I think that we must first tackle our own problem. We ought to find out what it was that swung Western Europe and America away, at the beginning of the twentieth century, and diverted the current that seemed to be flowing in the direction of a more profound level of cultural understanding of the Near East. If we could discover what that was, perhaps the discovery might help us to build up, with increasing sureness and mastery, a cultural program on the lines which Mr. Graves has presented, and to achieve what our predecessors, in the generation which immediately preceded mine, were evidently aiming at doing, but failed to do.*

* Charles P. Issawi remarked on this point: "The strongest motive force in human beings is fear, and my own reading of that period is that suddenly the West began to fear the East. Japan was industrializing. A very strong national consciousness was developing in those countries, and I frankly think the West just began to feel that the rising tide of color would engulf it."

II. THE NEAR EAST

J. C. HUREWITZ

The United Nations and Palestine

The Palestine problem, one of the most complicated international problems in our generation, has many aspects. As a natural consequence of the growing tension in and over Palestine, public discussion of this issue has in recent years fallen almost wholly into the class of polemics and apologetics. In these acrimonious debates most participants have sided with either the Arabs or the Jews, although the apologists for the policies—or lack of policy—of the United Kingdom, the United States, and the Soviet Union have not been silent. In all of the shouting there has been a tendency either to ignore or to play down the United Nations role in dealing with Palestine. It is to this subject—to explaining the achievements and failures of the United Nations in Palestine—that I address myself. Any views I may express are entirely my own. In no way do they represent the position of the United Nations Secretariat, with which I was happy to be associated until quite recently.

The handling of the Palestine problem has involved the use of a wider variety of procedures and engaged more organs than has, so far, any other political question before the United Nations. The methods of pacific settlement to which the United Nations has resorted in connection with Palestine have included investigation, attempted administration and trusteeship, truce and armistice negotiations and supervision, mediation and conciliation, refugee relief, and economic survey and rehabilitation. Four principal organs—the General Assembly, the Security Council, the Trusteeship Council, and the Economic and Social Council—have, in the idiom of Lake Success, been "seized of" various phases of this problem. Of some twenty-three commissions or subsidiary organs created by the General Assembly and the Security Council to deal with political disputes, ten have been established in connection with Palestine.[1] Moreover, five specialized agencies of the United Nations—FAO, IRO, UNESCO, UNICEF, and WHO *—have contributed in varying measure to the relief programs for Palestine refugees. In conjunction with this elaborate effort documentation has accumulated which is literally overwhelming.[2] I shall therefore have to limit myself to a selective survey.

The United Nations, it should be stressed at the very outset, did not create the Palestine problem. It came to Lake Success full-blown, far beyond the stage of reasonable and peaceful adjustment. In Palestine itself a triangular struggle raged between Arabs and Jews and between each and the British. The struggle produced repercussions in the near-by Arab states, all of which had actively endorsed the cause of the Palestine Arabs; and among Jews the world over, particularly those in Europe, the British dominions, and the Americas, the overwhelming majority of whom supported the cause of the Jewish National Home. By reason of the presence in Palestine of shrines holy to Christianity, Islam, and Judaism, the contest had also acquired religious overtones. But most serious of all was the involvement of the Palestine problem in the power politics of the Big Three. As long as the United Kingdom was a party to the dispute, it was only natural that the United States and the Soviet Union should also be drawn in, particularly because of the contracting British commitments in the Near East as a whole since the close of World War II. This sharpened the rivalry in the area between Washington and Moscow, for each seemed determined to prevent the other from filling the power-political vacuum.

---

* Food and Agriculture Organization; International Refugee Organization; United Nations Educational, Social, Cultural Organization; United Nations International Children's Emergency Fund; World Health Organization.

This was the problem which the United Nations inherited when Great Britain first placed the item on the agenda of the General Assembly in the spring of 1947.[3]

The United Nations' handling of the Palestine question may be said to have passed, thus far, through three distinct but overlapping phases, each of more than one year's duration: the abortive attempt peacefully to divide the territory into Arab and Jewish states; the successful localization and termination of the war to which the mandate's expiry gave rise; and the efforts, inconclusive as yet, to reach a final peace settlement.

The first period lasted from the opening of the first special session (28 April—15 May 1947) of the General Assembly through the demise of the Palestine Mandate on 14 May 1948. From the start it was clear that the mandate would have to go, for this was an outmoded instrument of the League of Nations. What then was to take its place? Was the mandate to be superseded by a trusteeship, as the Anglo-American Inquiry Committee had recommended a year earlier? Or was Palestine to be granted its independence? If the latter, was the territory to remain under a unitary government? If so, was it to be an Arab or a Jewish or a federated Arab-Jewish state? Or was the land to be parceled into separate Arab and Jewish countries? To help find the appropriate answer, the General Assembly at its first special session established an investigative body called the United Nations Special Committee on Palestine, or UNSCOP, with instructions to make a fresh assemblage of the facts and to submit recommendations for consideration at the second regular session.[4]

At that session (16 September—29 November 1947) the Assembly adopted, with some modification, the proposal of UNSCOP's majority to partition Palestine into Arab and Jewish states which were to remain in economic union and to create a special international regime for the City of Jerusalem. The execution of the scheme was entrusted to a subsidiary organ called the United Nations Palestine Commission or UNPAC, consisting of five smaller nations, selected on the principle of geographic distribution, so as to insure its neutrality. The Assembly requested the Security Council to determine as a threat to the peace, breach of the peace, or act of aggression any attempt forcibly to alter the proposed settlement and, if it were decided that such a threat existed, to take appropriate action under Chapter VII of the United Nations Charter. The Assembly also called upon the Trusteeship Council to draft within five months a detailed statute for the projected Jerusalem regime and upon the Economic and Social Council to elect the three foreign members of a Joint Economic Board which was intended to supervise the proposed Arab-Jewish economic union.[5]

As is well known, the Assembly's partition resolution was never implemented. A small advance Secretariat party did reach Jerusalem early in March 1948. But UNPAC's members, who never left Lake Success, were jokingly labeled at the time "the five lonely pilgrims," and the rumor circulated that, if these "pilgrims" ever left for Palestine, they would be provided only with one-way passage. The reasons for UNPAC's failure were many. The United Kingdom, determined to have no part in the territorial division of Palestine, refused to accept the Assembly's recommendations or to coöperate with the Commission. So, too, did the Palestine Arab Community and the near-by Arab states.[6] Most important, however, was the effective neutralization of the United Nations in the early spring of 1948 as a result of the rivalry among the Big Three. With the intensification of the East-West "cold war," mutual suspicions were too strong to allow for any real measure of collaboration. Moreover, Washington and London were also moving in different directions. The United States, which had endorsed the partition proposal without qualification the previous fall, attempted to reverse its position in the spring of 1948 by advocating a temporary trusteeship. This about-face weakened American prestige among the smaller powers, whose support was indispensable for the adoption of such a proposal, and failed to elicit the backing of the United Kingdom, which resisted—both in the Security Council and in the second special session of the General Assembly—American suggestions for even a brief extension of Palestine's tutelary status.[7]

In the end, the United Nations virtually lost all control over the situation in Palestine. The civil war which broke out in December 1947 between the local Arab Community, with the aid of volunteers from the surrounding Arab lands, and the Jewish Community, with technical and financial assistance from American and European Jews, began markedly to favor the Palestine Jews after mid-April 1948. Moreover, the Jewish Community proceeded with its plans— until 17 April 1948 in consultation with UNPAC—for the formation of a Provisional Government and on 14 May announced the establishment of the state of Israel. By midnight on the same day the British laid down their mandate. Though the first phase of the United Nations handling of the Palestine problem closed amid chaos, there were nevertheless two positive achievements. The Palestine Jews were enabled to attain their sovereignty and the British to extricate themselves from an impossible situation.

The second United Nations phase—which sought to prevent the war from spreading and, if possible, to end the hostilities altogether —really began before the termination of the mandate. The Security Council issued three appeals in March and April 1948 for a cease-fire and for the negotiation of a truce. These were followed on 23 April by the establishment of a Truce Commission for Palestine composed of the career consuls in Jerusalem of Belgium, France, and the United States.[8] These appeals and the efforts of the Truce Commission, however, were unavailing. Furthermore, while the General Assembly at its second special session (16 April—14 May 1948) refused either to revoke its earlier partition resolution or to adopt the United States proposal calling for a temporary trusteeship, it nevertheless dissolved UNPAC and provided for the selection by the Big Five of a United Nations Mediator in Palestine, among other purposes, to "promote a peaceful adjustment of the future situation of Palestine" and to coöperate with the Security Council's Truce Commission.[9] But on 15 May "the Palestine situation" deteriorated rapidly, owing to the Arab League states' military intervention with the avowed objectives of destroying, the nascent Jewish state before it could take secure root and handing over governmental authority in the territory to the Palestine Arabs.[10] On 20 May announcement was made of the appointment of Count Folke Bernadotte, the president of the Swedish Red Cross, as United Nations Mediator.

Chief responsibility for containing the spreading war now devolved upon the Security Council. But in this organ Anglo-American differences over Palestine at first precluded the adoption of any effective decision. President Truman, it will be recalled, extended *de facto* recognition to the Provisional Government of Israel shortly after it had come into existence. The United Kingdom for its part was still sending arms to Egypt, Iraq, and Transjordan, allegedly in pursuance of its treaty arrangements with these three countries. Thus, on 17 May the United States introduced in the Security Council a draft resolution, declaring that the situation in Palestine constituted a breach of the peace within the meaning of Article 39 of the Charter and ordering a cease-fire within 36 hours. Two days later the United Kingdom submitted an amendment, eliminating the reference to Article 39. The resolution, as amended, was adopted on 22 May and, needless to add, was fruitless, owing to the studied omission of any reference to Chapter VII of the Charter or to the possible use of economic and military sanctions for which that chapter provides.[11]

At this point American public opinion became aroused against the United Kingdom, threatening suspension of the American loan to Britain, which, if it occurred, would have undermined the Economic Coöperation Administration, then just getting under way. At the end of a week of sustained American pressure, the British Government finally backed down and agreed to stop its arms shipments to the Arab states and its subsidization of the Arab Legion in Transjordan. This enabled the Security Council to adopt on 29 May a resolution with teeth. The parties were called upon to order a four-week cease-fire and to stop the importation of war matériel and fighting personnel into Palestine or the Arab countries. The Security Council directed the Mediator in common with the Truce Commission to supervise the observance of these provisions and warned that the situation in Palestine would be reconsidered with a view to action under Chapter VII, if the resolution were rejected or violated by one or more of the parties.[12] Count Bernadotte was very fortunate in the support which he thus received from the Security Council and in the assistance which the Secretariat provided him in the person of Dr. Ralph J. Bunche, who had by this time acquired an intimate knowledge of the Palestine problem through his earlier association with UNSCOP and UNPAC. But, above all, Count Bernadotte brought to the task his vibrant personality, his prestige, and his perseverance. The Mediator—whose over-all responsibility for the negotiations was acknowledged by the Truce Commission—was thus able to arrange the first truce, which went into effect on 11 June.

The time, however, was still not ripe for a general armistice, let alone a final political settlement. Consequently, the Mediator's political proposals, put forward in the third week of the truce, were turned down by both sides. In the following week, when it appeared that fighting might be resumed, the Mediator and the Security Council appealed to the parties to prolong the truce. This appeal was accepted in principle by Israel but rejected by the Arab states.[13] The explanation is fairly clear in retrospect. The Arab states, after all, did have initial superiority over Israel in arms and in regularly trained armed forces. Israel had little heavy military equipment at the start, and it faced such serious basic problems as the need for setting up its governmental machinery and transforming its secret militia into a regular army. Nevertheless if Israel entertained any fears about its ability to cope with the military situation, these proved unfounded in the six days of fighting which ensued after the expiry of the first truce. The Israel Army seized the initiative and, in the central sector, widened the Israel corridor to Jerusalem.

The Security Council, on the advice of the Mediator who had returned to Lake Success to report in person, adopted on 15 July its most strongly worded resolution up to that time. The Council determined that the situation in Palestine constituted a threat to the peace within the meaning of Article 39; ordered the parties to conclude an indefinite truce, to take effect in Jerusalem within twenty-four hours and in the rest of Palestine within three days; and warned that noncompliance would lead to further action under Chapter VII of the Charter.[14] In the wake of this resolution general hostilities ceased. But both sides continued to violate the truce, particularly in the Jerusalem area. Indeed, many of the Jewish terrorists of mandatory days had assembled here for the purpose of avoiding the jurisdiction of the Provisional Government of Israel and annexing the city to the new state. It was in Jerusalem that terrorists associated with the Fighters for Israel's Freedom or the so-called Stern Gang assassinated Count Bernadotte on 17 September. Dr. Bunche was now named Acting Mediator.

Dissatisfaction with the truce lines was stronger among the Israelis than among the Arabs. At this time Israel controlled the coastal plain from a point below Jaffa, the Jezreel valley, eastern Galilee, and the corridor to Jerusalem. The Israelis were determined to incorporate into their state the Negeb, which, despite the few Jewish settlements in the district, was in the hands of the Egyptian and Transjordan forces. When the Egyptian Army afforded a pretext by refusing to allow an Israel convoy to proceed to Jewish villages in the Negeb, the Israel Army undertook to clear the Egyptians out of that area. This was accomplished in two stages, at the end of October and again at the end of December. Also in October, the Lebanese troops were driven out of central Galilee, and a portion of southeastern Lebanon was occupied. Of these military actions the most decisive was that against Egypt at the turn of the year. The Israel offensive, which began on 22 December 1948, carried advance units across the Egyptian border. The adamant refusal of Cairo to invoke its treaty of 1936 with the United Kingdom and to seek British military assistance coupled with the seriously unsettled conditions in Egypt itself, which had resulted in the murder on 29 December of Prime Minister Mahmud Fahmi Pasha al-Nuqrashi, induced the Egyptian Government to agree to armistice negotiations.[15]

Egypt and Israel sent delegations to the headquarters of the Acting Mediator on the island of Rhodes, where the talks commenced on 12 January 1949. It was here that Dr. Bunche displayed his patience, skill, and energy in keeping the delegations from leaving the conference table and furnishing draft after draft of each controversial provision until the first armistice agreement was signed on 24 February. This was followed by similar agreements between Israel and Lebanon on 22 March, between Israel and what now came to be known as Jordan on 3 April, and finally between Israel and Syria on 20 July.[16] Iraq had already stated that it would accept the armistice terms agreeable to Palestine's immediate Arab neighbors, and Saudi Arabia that it would abide by the decision which had been or might be adopted by the Arab League. Meanwhile, early in March, soon after the start of the Israel-Transjordan talks, Israel troops had moved down the eastern part of the Negeb, forcing the withdrawal of the token Arab Legion troops. The armistice agreements left Israel in *de facto* possession of most of the Negeb, the coastal plain, the corridor to Jerusalem, and Galilee. Israel troops evacuated southeastern Lebanon; the Egyptian Army retained control over the Gaza strip; and, following the withdrawal of the Iraqi units from central Palestine in March 1949, this area was left to Jordan military administration. The armistice agreements also provided for the establishment of four Mixed Armistice Commissions, each under the neutral chairmanship of the Chief of Staff of the United Nations Truce Supervision Organization, then Brigadier-General William E. Riley of the U.S.M.C. On 11 August 1949 the Security Council, taking cognizance of the four armistice agreements, terminated the office of the Mediator but provided for the continuation of the Truce Supervision Organization to assist the Mixed Armistice Commissions in implementing the agreements.[17] By this act the second phase of the United Nations handling of the Palestine problem came to a successful conclusion.

The third phase, that which is still with us, has concerned chiefly the efforts to reach a final peace settlement and began during the first part of the General Assembly's third regular session (21 September—12 December 1948). The decisions on Palestine taken by the Assembly at that session were based largely on proposals in the posthumous Progress Report of Count Bernadotte.[18] The report made two recommendations of special interest to that organ. One related to the care of the then estimated half million Palestine Arab refugees, who had been displaced either by factors attending the termination of the mandate or by the war to which it gave rise. Following a request of the Arab League as early as July 1948, the Mediator had inaugurated, with the coöperation of the United Nations specialized agencies as well as voluntary welfare and religious societies, a provisional relief program. The Mediator now urged that the United Nations assume formal responsibility for care of the displaced Arabs. This scheme was adopted by the Assembly on 19 November 1948, when it set up the United

Nations Relief for Palestine Refugees or UNRPR, which took over from the Acting Mediator the entire refugee program. UNRPR's budget of some $32 millions was to be raised by voluntary governmental contributions.[19] Stanton Griffis, former American Ambassador to Egypt, was named director, and about 50 per cent of the total budget was underwritten by the United States Government.

The Mediator's second recommendation concerned the mediation and truce supervision efforts. In the late summer of 1948 Count Bernadotte had begun to feel that perhaps he had exhausted his usefulness following the arrangement of the truces, and that it might be preferable to entrust the mediation and truce supervision functions, which were so closely interrelated, to a conciliation commission. This proposal was later fully endorsed by the Acting Mediator. Accordingly, the Assembly on 11 December adopted a resolution providing for the establishment of the United Nations Conciliation Commission for Palestine. On the same day France, Turkey, and the United States were designated as its members. The Commission was instructed to assist the parties "to achieve a final settlement of all questions outstanding between them." The Assembly also contemplated that the Security Council would transfer to the Conciliation Commission all of the functions which the Council had assigned to the Mediator and to its own Truce Commission, so as to integrate these activities in one body.[20]

But the member states of the Conciliation Commission were tardy in appointing their representatives. By the time the latter were ready to assume active duty at the end of January 1949, Dr. Bunche was already seated at the conference table with Egypt and Israel. In order not to jeopardize the armistice talks, as the transfer of this effort from the Acting Mediator to the untried Conciliation Commission might have done, Bunche was allowed to carry on and the new body addressed itself solely to the realization of a final peace settlement.[21] Admittedly, the achievement of this objective has presented the most difficult problems. Still the Conciliation Commission proceeded to blunder in its own right. It embarked upon its activities before it had an opportunity of profiting from Bunche's productive experience with armistice negotiations. It had no real comprehension of its assignment: for the longest time the Commission regarded its primary function as that of good offices—that is, of persuading the parties (in this case, chiefly the Arabs) to treat with each other directly—instead of conciliation—that is, not only of bringing the parties together but of taking an active part in the actual negotiations. As a result, the Commission has tended to be timid when it should have been bold, and obdurate when it should have been flexible. Obviously, neither France nor Turkey could take the lead, yet the two governments sought in vain for guidance from Washington. This was due in part to the continued ambivalent attitude toward Palestine on the part of the United States Government, which alternated its sympathies and favors between Israel and the Arab states, instead of following an independent and consistent policy. It also derived from the initial inability of the United States to find a representative who was willing to devote himself to the Commission's work. Washington appointed four successive representatives in less than a year. The first resigned before reaching the field; the second left immediately after the opening contacts with the parties were made; the third remained for just a few months; and finally the United States had to resort to appointing a career diplomat to assure that there would be no further turnover.

In these circumstances it is little wonder that the Conciliation Commission has made very little headway toward its goal. In its primary task of arranging a final peace, the Commission has passed from deadlock to deadlock. The Arab states have insisted on the absolute priority of the refugee question as a prerequisite to the consideration of any other question. Israel has adamantly maintained that it would review the refugee question only as a part of the negotiations for a final settlement of all questions. The Arab states have refused to have any direct contact with Israel or to deal with the Commission except as a group. Israel, on the other hand, has been pressing for direct parleys, preferably with each Arab state individually. Consequently, aside from the Economic Survey Mission, which will be examined presently, the Conciliation Commission has made progress only in peripheral matters, such as the reuniting in Israel of refugee families separated by the war or "unfreezing" blocked assets.[22] The Commission's failure in Jerusalem followed a similar pattern. The Commission had been instructed to present to the fourth session of the General Assembly in 1949 a draft instrument for an international regime in Jerusalem. This draft was indeed prepared. But the Commission failed to win the approval for its scheme of Israel and Jordan, the two powers in *de facto* possession of the Holy City; and the Assembly itself proceeded to by-pass the Commission's recommendations by adopting an even more drastic proposal for the permanent internationalization of the Jerusalem area. The Trusteeship Council, which had been directed to frame the statute for this purpose, went through the mechanical motions of doing so; but owing to the continued opposition of Israel and Jordan, decided in June 1950 to return the question to the General Assembly.[23]

The Conciliation Commission's one major and at least partly successful undertaking lay in the economic sphere. The General Assembly had originally directed the Commission to devise a program for promoting the economic development of the area affected by the Palestine war and to facilitate the repatriation, resettlement, and economic and social rehabilitation of the refugees. In this connection, the Commission formed in August 1949 an Economic Survey Mission for the Middle East. On the basis of the Mission's recommendations to the General Assembly, a United Nations Relief and Works Agency for Palestine Refugees in the Near East was established in December 1949 to replace the UNRPR and to lead the refugees away from the dole to productive economic activity. With a budget of $54.9 millions, to be raised by voluntary governmental subscription, it was hoped that the Relief and Works Agency could employ large numbers of displaced Arabs in the countries where they were chiefly to be found—Jordan, Lebanon, and Syria—on various pilot projects. Through this means it was believed that the two purposes of aiding the refugees and bolstering the economies of the Arab states might be achieved simultaneously.[24] It is still too early to tell what results the Relief and Works Agency will be able to report. Nevertheless, the prolonged delay before the agency could start its program was bound to have a negative influence. Indeed, here was an excellent example of the difficulty of finding competent personnel to take on the thankless

ɔbs of working on the Palestine problem. Some twenty-six can-
ɪidates had been approached before Major-General Howard Ken-
ɪedy of Canada finally accepted in March 1950 the post of director
ɪf the Relief and Works Agency.

This, in brief, is an outline of the major activities of the United
ɪations in Palestine. Palestine remains on the active list of po-
ɪitical problems before the international organization. A final judg-
ɪnent of the record must wait until such time as the question has
ɪinally been removed from the agenda of the principal organs of
ɪhe United Nations.

Nevertheless, the accomplishments to date, while mixed, have
ɪeen substantial. To recapitulate: the Palestine problem was al-
ɪeady incapable of rational solution by the time it reached Lake
ɪuccess. While the United Nations could not therefore arrive at a
ɪecision acceptable to all, at least the Palestine Jews were enabled
ɪo establish their independent state and the British to lay down
ɪheir mandate. The United Nations could not prevent the outbreak
ɪf war, but it did manage to restrict the area of combat and lead
ɪhe belligerents first to a truce and then to a binding armistice.
We seem at this juncture to be as far as possible from a final po-
ɪitical settlement, but the United Nations has at least placed in the
ɪield an instrument for the negotiation of such a settlement and, in
ɪhe interim, has called the attention of the international commu-
ɪity to its responsibility for the care of the Palestine refugees.

NOTES

1. Three commissions each were created in connection with the questions of Greece, Indonesia, and India-Pakistan; two each in connection
with Korea and the former Italian Colonies. The ten commissions on
Palestine were the following: the United Nations Special Committee on
Palestine (UNSCOP), the United Nations Palestine Commission (UNPAC),
the Security Council Truce Commission for Palestine, the United Na-
tions Special Municipal Commissioner for Jerusalem, the United Nations
Mediator (and Acting Mediator) in Palestine, the United Nations Relief
for Palestine Refugees, the United Nations Conciliation Commission for
Palestine, the United Nations Truce Supervision Organization, the United
Nations Economic Survey Mission for the Middle East, and the United
Nations Relief and Works Agency for Palestine Refugees in the Near
East.

2. A continuing summary of the United Nations record in Palestine may be found in the *Annual Report of the Secretary-General on the Work of the Organization;* the 2nd-5th reports (documents A/315, A/565, A/930, and A/1287) contain data on Palestine. These reports should be used, not as the final source of information, but as a convenient guide to the study of the *Official Records.* As regards the General Assembly, it is necessary only to make note, in the Secretary-General's reports, of the Committee to which the question was referred at each session and of the numbers of the Plenary Meetings; this will save considerable time in tracking down the appropriate *Official Records* of the General Assembly. The pertinent resolutions may be found in documents A/310, A/519, A/555, A/810, A/900, and A/1251. The Secretary-General's reports also provide the date on which the Economic and Social Council and the Trusteeship Council dealt with the Palestine question, although in connection with the most recent work of the Trusteeship Council on Jerusalem (8 December 1949–14 June 1950) it is best to consult the Council's special report on the *Question of an International Regime for the Jerusalem Area and Protection of the Holy Places* (document A/1286). The *Official Records* of the Security Council are perhaps the most difficult for the uninitiated to use. For this reason it is essential to refer to the annual *Report of the Security Council to the General Assembly,* which serves as a substantive index to the meetings and documents of this permanent organ. The two reports (documents A/620 and A/945) for the period between 16 July 1947 and 15 July 1949 furnish a substantive index to the wealth of material relating to Palestine. The only subsequent documents of importance are: the *Official Records of the Security Council,* fourth year, Nos. 36–38, 46, and 49; *Supplement for August 1949; Special Supplement No. 2;* resolution of 11 August 1949 (S/1376); and the most recent complaints to the Secretary-General by the Arab states and Israel (documents S/1631, S/1640, S/1648, S/1650, S/1654, and S/1660). The document numbers of the reports to the Security Council by the Palestine Commission, the Truce Commission, and the Mediator (and Acting Mediator) are contained in the annual report of the Security Council mentioned above, while the document numbers of the reports to the General Assembly by the remaining commissions may be found in the appropriate Committee records. The *Final Report of the United Nations Economic Survey Mission for the Middle East* was published on 28 December 1949 (2 vols., document A/AC.25/6). The only public report to date of the Chief of Staff of the Truce Supervision Organization is S/1459. The Special Municipal Commissioner for Jerusalem, who never reached his destination in the field, did not issue any reports. The internal records of the several commissions are still restricted and therefore are not generally available. On the other hand, the Secretariat has published, for the use of the Interim Committee of the General Assembly (Sub-Committee on International Co-operation in the Political Field) memoranda on the *Organization and Procedure of United Nations Commissions.* Of the eleven pamphlets which have thus far appeared, the following four deal with Palestine: III (UNSCOP), VII (UNPAC), IX (Truce Commission), and X (Mediator and Acting Mediator).

3. A/286.

4. Resolution 106(S–1).
5. Resolution 181(II).
6. Cf. UNPAC's report to the General Assembly, A/532, pp. 34–36.
7. See, for instance, *Official Records of the Security Council,* third year, No. 52, pp. 26–27 and 32–33; and *Official Records of the General Assembly,* second special session, II, 62–63, 209–211, and 218–219.
8. Resolutions S/691, S/714/I, S/723, and S/727.
9. Resolution 186(S–2).
10. S/745.
11. S/749 (U. S. draft resolution), S/755 (U. K. amendment), and /773 (resolution adopted by Security Council).
12. Resolution S/801.
13. S/875 (Security Council's resolution) and S/871, S/872, S/873, /876, and S/884 (attitudes of the Arab states and Israel).
14. Resolution S/902.
15. S/1187.
16. *Official Records of the Security Council,* fourth year, Special Supplements Nos. 1–4.
17. Resolution S/1376/II.
18. A/648.
19. Resolution 212(III).
20. Resolution 194(III).
21. A/819 (Conciliation Commission's first progress report).
22. Cf. later progress reports of the Conciliation Commission: A/838, A/927, A/973, A/1252, A/1255, and A/1288.
23. A/1286.
24. Resolution 302(IV).

MOSHE KEREN

Israel and the United States *

This article dwells briefly on the relations between Israel and the United States, with special emphasis on the future. It is not without hesitation that I undertake this task, not because the relations between our two democratic nations are unsatisfactory—on the contrary, they are entirely cordial and have every prospect, as I hope to show, of improving still more in the future course. But these relations cover an extremely wide field. They are in no way confined to political contacts in the strictest sense of the word. Close bonds exist between America and Israel in the cultural, social, and economic sphere, and these bonds are interrelated and interwoven. The traffic of goods has its impact on the traffic of thought and vice versa, and both influence and are part of the political relations. It is not easy to disentangle these different criss-crossing strands and then to weave them together again into a well-ordered picture.

Before I try to analyze the particular problems which arise out of the daily contact between the two countries, it might be useful to point to certain general features which characterize and give specific form to these relations.

First, the association between Israel and the United States is that between two free nations equal in sovereignty but vastly unequal, of course, in power and wealth. The relations between the United States and Israel are conducted on the basis of equality and independence where each partner is free to grant or to deny the requests of the other. On the other hand, it is only natural that this political equality does not and cannot under the present circumstances cancel out the immense difference of wealth and economic power be-

* These remarks refer to the situation as of the summer of 1950.

.ween the two countries. Like so many other nations, Israel looks to
America in many ways for a solution or an amelioration of its
serious economic difficulties, and I am happy to state that she has
enjoyed in the past generous support from both the American pub-
ic and the government.

Second, Israel is a modern secular democracy conforming in
general with the Western European pattern. She has a parliament
chosen in free elections, and a government dependent on the confidence of this parliament. Her citizens enjoy fully the right of free
speech and all those other liberties and duties of man which the
evolution of the last two centuries has bestowed upon progressive
and free societies. She thus resembles in many respects the old-
established industrialized liberal states of Western Europe, being
different from them only in her youthful vigor, her burning ambition to build and to develop, and, too, in her many and severe
growing pains. This characteristic of Israel as a liberal democratic
state gives her a natural affinity to the spirit of American democracy and defines her attitude in principle towards the great ideological conflict which today rips the world into two rivaling parts.

Third, Israel, in addition to being a liberal democracy, is a
Jewish State—the only Jewish State in existence. This fact throws
upon her a special set of problems and obligations, some of them
of awe-inspiring magnitude. Among them the problem of immigration takes precedence before all. Two thousand years of persecution and especially the terrible experiences of the recent past
have left their ineradicable impression on the Jewish mind. The
Jewish people in Israel feel they are responsible for the life of
every Jew who might be saved from persecution in the shelter of
Israel's shores. Public opinion in Israel demands therefore the right
of free and unlimited emigration for every Jew who wishes to enter
her gates. The people of Israel are willing to bear all the sacrifices
which this mass emigration entails, and they accept, therefore,
without grudge, a regime of drab austerity. But the burden of absorbing these immigrants has reached such dimensions that it cannot be borne by the people in Israel alone. The Jewish population
of Israel, which numbered about 650,000 at the time of the establishment of the State, has grown by almost 70 per cent to about

1,100,000 at the present moment. The task of absorption which Israel faces constitutes the major problem around which its whole economy centers. On the other hand the fact that Israel is predominantly Jewish creates a unique bond between her people and the great Jewish community of the United States which, after the virtual extinction of the Jewish centers of eastern Europe, represents by far the most numerous, the healthiest, and the wealthiest branch of the Jewish people.

Fourth, and finally, Israel is situated in one of the strategic regions of the globe, a region in whose peace and stability the United States has a direct and vital interest. She won her independence in an unequal but victorious struggle against the surrounding Arab States who invaded her soil in defiance of the will of the United Nations. Her Arab neighbors still view Israel with hostility. Although the actual fighting has been brought to an end by armistice treaties, the prospects of real peace in the near future are not very bright. The Arab States persist in their refusal to enter into direct negotiations for a final settlement. Tension prevails unabated, and so far the healing influence of time has hardly shown its effect. This unsatisfactory state of affairs creates many of the political problems which furnish the content of negotiation and exchange of views between your government and mine.

If you will allow me to analyze more closely these various elements which together form the basis of the relations between Israel and the United States, I might perhaps start with a very brief description of the bonds which link the people of Israel and the Jewish community in America. These relations are *sui generis,* the like of which do not, I believe, exist between any other country and its related community within the United States. The creation of the Jewish State evoked an upsurge of emotion which swept the Jewish community in America as everywhere else in the world. After the terrible depression caused by the unrevenged slaughter of the six million Jews in Europe, the establishment of Israel against great odds appears as a kind of vindication of Judaism before fate. The restoration of Jewish statehood after two thousand years, and the considerable share which American Jewry had in the creation of the new state, filled it with a new pride and self-assertion. Jewish

ganizations in this country almost without exception adopted a
definite pro-Israel policy. The sympathy with which American
Jewry followed the development of the Jewish State had most tangible results. It is without precedent, as far as I know, that voluntary organizations such as the United Jewish Appeal should collect
year after year sums to the tune of one hundred million dollars and
more, the major portion dedicated to purposes connected with
Israel. Besides this, the keen interest and support which American
Jewry rendered Israel on many occasions has had a most vital significance for Israel.

I have already mentioned the tremendous burden which the unprecedented scale of immigration has loaded upon the people of
Israel. Israel feels entitled to look for help outside her borders
since by receiving those hundreds of thousands she has fulfilled a
humanitarian task of international importance and contributed to
the solution of one of the most tragic problems of mankind, a share
quite out of proportion to her size and the scarcity of her means.
But in addition to the direct support which the people of Israel
have received from Jewish communities all over the world, other
considerable funds which cover at least a part of the capital import
needed have come from the United States. Israel has been granted
a loan of one hundred million dollars from the Export-Import
Bank, which plays a vital role in the development of the country
and in the enlargement of its absorptive capacity. Private investment too has flowed into Israel on a moderate but by no means
negligible scale. Kaiser-Fraser is erecting a factory for the assembly of trucks and cars. General Tire of Akron plans to start production of tires in Israel. Of other forms of support which we enjoy
from the generous people and government of the United States, I
might mention the purchase of potatoes from the Department of
Agriculture at a nominal price and the free grant of considerable
quantities of egg and milk powder, butter and cheese for charitable
purposes.

In addition to this, we have been ambitious to learn the secrets
of American know-how and have in this respect again invariably
found understanding and support. A mission of forty-four selected
workers of various industries visited your country for several weeks

a short while ago and learned firsthand the technique of productio
and organization. American experts of top rank, like Dr. Walte
Lowdermilk and Mr. Savage, have been consulted by my goverr
ment in their related fields. An educational mission will be sent i
the near future by your government to mine in order to render
report on our educational efforts and problems. Many hundreds c
students study in American universities in all branches of know
edge. Under the Smith-Mundt Act, two leading personalities i
our public life, the Vice-Mayor of Tel Aviv and the Secretary c
our Knesset (parliament), are at present in the United States i
order to compare your methods and achievements with our ow
problems and solutions in their respective fields of interest. A gue:
professor of international authority will shortly begin to teach i
the technical college of Haifa under the same auspices.

It is with this background of close contacts in the agricultura
and economic fields that our political relations with the Unite
States should be viewed. It is obvious that for Israel, her relation
with the United States constitute a most central point of her policy
The strengthening of our friendship with the government and peo
ple of the United States is one of the major aims of our statesman
ship. But I venture to say too, that owing to the manifold clos
contacts which exist between our two countries, and owing to the ap
peal which Israel's renaissance has to the imagination and gener
osity of the American public, our place in American policy is mucl
more important than the smallness of our country and the deartl
of our means would justify. This is not to say that our politica
relations have always been or will always remain free from prob
lems, but I believe firmly that it is possible to deal successfully witl
all these problems as they arise on the basis of an underlying sym
pathy and understanding. More than that, I am convinced of the
basic identity of the principal aims which govern the course o
policy in both nations. The two countries have a vital interest i
peace, both in the world in general and in the Near East in par
ticular. The government of the United States has repeatedly an
nounced that the reëstablishment of peace and stability in the Nea
East is the leading goal of all its political actions. The same is true
with respect to the government of Israel. We firmly believe tha

the present state of tension and instability is to the detriment of the region as a whole and that the entire area cannot develop and progress so long as the present dissension and rivalry prevail. There is no problem between Israel and the Arab States which could not ultimately be solved in direct and frank negotiations, and we hold the obstinate refusal on the part of the Arabs even to enter into such negotiations as a wholly indefensible breach of the obligations which every State has towards the community of nations.

Israel's policy is aligned with the United Nations. We, like you, believe that the ultimate redemption of the world from its present anxieties and dangers lies with the establishment of a firm and democratic order among nations. We as a small and weak nation view with dread the possibility of a third holocaust with its prospects of limitless destruction for all. It was with this belief in the need for reasserting the supremacy of international law and order that the government of Israel decided to support the United Nations action in Korea and to side with the common front against aggression. In order to give practical expression to its stand on the Korean issue, my government has come forward with an offer of medical aid to the United Nations forces in Korea. Israel, which has been a victim of aggression, knows from her own bitter experience that chaos would result if aggression were to go unopposed and unpunished.

I would, however, not be frank were I to fail to make clear that in certain respects Israel has maintained an independent line in the world struggle. Israel has adopted the policy not to identify herself *a priori* with one of the conflicting camps and she holds to her right, which is the right of every sovereign State, to judge each issue on its own merits. She has therefore occasionally taken a different stand from that of the United States on questions which came up in the Assembly, and she is anxious to keep normal relations with the Eastern bloc. We should not forget that a Jewry of several million lives in the Soviet Union and in the various countries which are affiliated with the Soviet Union. Israel as a Jewish State cannot afford to lose contact with so great and valuable a part of the Jewish people, and she is bound to strive with all diplomatic means in her power for the right of these Jews to emigrate to Israel. This policy has been in part, though by no means completely, successful. A continuous emigration has been maintained of Jews into Israel from the countries of Eastern Europe, but millions of Jews still continue to live there and their presence constitutes a bond which no government of Israel could sever lightheartedly.

On the other hand, as I have said before, the social and political character of Israel is similar to that of the Western powers. Communism is a negligible force in Israel. Her economic and cultural contacts are overwhelmingly with the West. If the government of Israel reserves for itself the right to evaluate each issue on its merits, the decision on the Korean war is a sufficient proof that Israel will in independent and free deliberation always align herself against aggression and on behalf of international peace and order.

I have tried to the best of my ability to analyze the elements of which our present relations with the United States are composed. I am optimistic that the tie of friendship between our two democratic nations will grow stronger year after year. My optimism is not based solely on these facts and reasons which I have given so far but on another factor which I have not yet mentioned. Israel is the only genuinely progressive and democratic state in a region which is suffering gravely from social retardation and underdevelopment. Israel is singularly free from those social vices which curb the development of so many nations around the globe and which haunt especially the Near East. She has no feudal or semi-feudal system, no wealthy landed class or underprivileged, impoverished masses. She has no illiteracy worth speaking of. Her democratic system is genuine and corresponds with the traditions and the will of her people. She is very far from perfect, but she is willing and able to learn and improve. In contrast to her stagnant surroundings, she is a dynamic, bustling community. The devoted patriotism of her population is not directed against the outside world, does not hanker after foreign territory, but is tuned to the building up, the fertilization and development, of its own country. It is on this fact that I place my greatest hope for the continued improvement of the relations between your country and mine.

It was unavoidable perhaps that the birth of a dynamic and ever-changing community should prove to be a deeply disturbing factor in a static region. Many of the political difficulties which we have experienced in our contacts with other governments might stem from a traditional and deep-rooted aversion to such change of the *status quo,* of which Israel by her very existence is doubtless guilty. But I hope we will prove in the long run that the rise of Israel as a modern, non-feudal power will be to the blessing of the entire region. Recent history has proved that the Near East in its present stage of backwardness and poverty represents one of the trouble spots of international policy. The future of the Near East lies in the unity and coöperation of all its nations towards improving the standard of living. Israel is willing to work hand in hand with her neighbors for the common goal, and she believes that the logic of the situation will work ultimately in her favor. She is confident that in doing so she will have the close support of the United States.

RALPH BUNCHE

The Palestine Problem

I had my first experience with the Near East in June 1947 when I went out with the original United Nations Commission on Palestine, UNSCOP as it was known—the commission that subsequently recommended partition to the General Assembly of the United Nations. All of my experience has been in the realm of United Nations interest, which has not been political or economic but has been directed exclusively to the achievement of peace in that area. So I do not wish any misunderstanding in regard to any comments that I may make. They will be made as the comments of a layman on this subject and necessarily will be concerned with the United Nations in the Near East.

With regard to oil, I may say that fortunately oil did not figure prominently in any of the United Nations negotiations or mediation efforts in connection with the Palestine conflict. Never once in the course of our negotiations with Arabs and Israelis was any mention made of oil either to Count Bernadotte or to myself. It may well have been that oil figured in the policies of great powers, of certain of them which were concerned with the settlement of the Palestine problem, but it was something that never crossed our path and we were very happy about it. Had it done so; had oil been found in the Negev, then the Palestine problem would probably have been impossible of solution. I recall that very often Israeli friends, with whom I talked unofficially, would say quite fervently that they were extremely happy that oil had not been found in the Negev. Things being as they are in this day and age, in their determined efforts to set up a state, which could only be small and relatively weak, their chances for real independence would diminish to the extent to which there might be promise of oil in their land.

I should mention that on one occasion a representation was made to us by one of the great powers with regard to the Haifa oil refineries, then under Israeli control but not operating during the period of the truce—and indeed not operating yet—and this representation was made in the terms of the world interest in, and need for, the refined oil which normally passed through at that time the largest refinery in that area. Count Bernadotte did make some effort to get those refineries in operation under conditions which would not have made the oil available to either side in the conflict, but which would have made it available to the world. But the pipeline came from Iraq and it was not possible to get oil flowing.

We were very fortunate in our work in Palestine, in a sort of negative sense, in three ways. First, that oil did not figure directly in the negotiations and was not therefore a stumbling block, and second that religion did not figure in the negotiations. Religion really did not figure in the conflict; it was not a religious war. Perhaps if it had been such it would still be going on. Finally, there was division in the United Nations on the Palestine question, but the division in the United Nations fortunately was not a division with regard to the problem of East and West and the "Cold War." The division cut across these lines very severely and I say that advisedly because in my memory, in the United Nations, this has been the only major issue on which in fact the Eastern Bloc itself was divided. This happened before the splitting off of Yugoslavia from the Soviet group and the Yugoslavs did not vote consistently with the other states associated with the Soviet Union on this question. Of course as far as the West was concerned, the Western states were greatly divided.

In regard to another question, it did seem quite apparent to me that despite the increasing oil production and the glittering figures in connection with it, the wealth derived from it has not found real reflection in the Near East. It remains an extremely poor area, an area in which poverty is strikingly widespread. I realize of course that the oil production is confined to two or three of the states, but the area generally is poor, desperately poor.

When we consider great power interest in the Near East as expressed through the United Nations, it is well to bear in mind certain misconceptions with regard to the role of the United Nations in connection with the Palestine conflict. The United Nations did not intervene in Near Eastern affairs voluntarily or on its own initiative. It was requested to intervene by the mandatory power, the United Kingdom, which asked the United Nations for assistance in dealing with this problem that had proved insoluble for the mandatory power. So in the spring of 1947, in response to the specific request of the United Kingdom, the United Nations convened in a special session of the General Assembly to deal with this problem. This led in turn to the partition, a decision which was never advanced as an ideal decision but as the only practical decision in the circumstances. It was a decision that caused a great deal of grief for the United Nations and for the Near East, since it led to violence. It led to open conflict and required a tremendous effort on the part of the United Nations to restore even a troubled and insecure peace to that area.

In connection with this subject of great power interest, there is one other misconception that I might take occasion to clear up. There were widespread stories in connection with the report which Count Bernadotte submitted to the General Assembly in the form of suggestions for the solution of the Palestine problem when that Assembly met in Paris in the fall of 1948. I recall that there was a full article on it—allegedly one that could be documented—in an important American periodical, to the effect that Count Bernadotte, who had been generally pictured in some circles as a tool of the British, was an instrument of the United States, and particularly the Wall Street part of the United States, and subservient to its interests. It was further stated that his report was in fact invented and prepared in the State Department. These rumors were given so much credence that in the course of the debate on Count Bernadotte's report in Paris at the General Assembly, one of the delegates quoted one of these printed articles as evidence of the fact that Count Bernadotte, whose report was being discussed posthumously, had been acting at the instance of London and Washington. The fact is, and I can vouch for it since I had a very close hand in it, that every word of the report was prepared by myself and my staff on the Island of Rhodes after full consultation with Count Bernadotte.

We began the preparation of the report on Friday the 10th of September 1948, just after we had returned from a visit to Alexandria and Tel Aviv. We had a staff of senior advisers of which I was in charge, consisting of a South African, Mr. Reedman, a Professor of Economics; Mr. Stavropulous, a former member of the diplomatic service in Greece; and Mr. Vigier, a Frenchman who had spent many years in the League of Nations. We had the first draft ready on Sunday the 12th. We sat down with Count Bernadotte beginning at four o'clock in the afternoon until five o'clock Monday morning, going over every word of it and working out compromise versions. There was never a complete agreement among us on certain phases of it, particularly those having to do with Galilee, Jerusalem, and the Negev, but the report came out as a compromise. Now what happened was that on Monday the 13th, two visitors landed on the Island of Rhodes without prior announcement to Count Bernadotte. They did not come together; they came in separate planes. One happened to be an officer of the State Department, and not a senior officer. The other happened to be an Englishman from the British Embassy in Cairo. They came officially for the purpose, and they had papers to show it, of discussing with Count Bernadotte proposals dealing with the problem of Arab refugees. It happened, perhaps unfortunately, that they came at the time, the last week in fact before Count Bernadotte's death, when we were preparing the report. We had part three of the report which dealt with the refugee question and this part three, then in first draft, was handed to these two gentlemen to read on the Island of Rhodes. Parts one and two were not handed to them; they dealt with the political aspects of the report. Subsequently those facts came to be magnified and distorted to read that the report itself had been prepared in Washington, had been checked and agreed upon by the British, and had been flown to Rhodes to be handed to Count Bernadotte for his reproduction and presentation to the General Assembly of the United Nations. I may say only that those of us on the staff who slaved on that report for five days, who got it ready on the 16th of September just before Count Bernadotte

117

took off for his final trip to Jerusalem before his assassination, resented very strongly these false stories, not only because of the way in which they dealt unjustly with a great internationalist, a man who had sacrificed his life in the cause of peace in Palestine, but also because of the effort we ourselves had put into that report.

E. L. DE GOLYER

Some Aspects of Oil in the Middle East

INTRODUCTION

Middle Eastern oil has become increasingly important in international affairs during recent years. It first attracted attention in 1914 when, upon the motion of Winston Churchill, then First Lord of Admiralty in the Asquith cabinet, the British Government purchased a majority interest in Anglo-Persian Oil Company, Ltd., owner of an oil concession over all of Persia except the northern provinces. Oil had been discovered in 1908, a pipe line completed by 1911, and a refinery built and in operation at the tidewater terminal of Abadan by 1912.

It was again in the limelight in 1920 when the British and French by the San Remo agreement of April 25 partitioned the oil rights of Mesopotamia—now Iraq—without providing for any possibility of participation by American interests. Diplomatic exchanges resulted in negotiations between interested companies from 1922 to 1928 and an agreement in the latter year by which a group of American companies secured a 23¾ per cent participation in Turkish Petroleum Company, Ltd., now Iraq Petroleum Company, Ltd.

The cancelation of the Anglo-Persian concession by Reza Shah Pahlavi in 1932 was another incident demanding world notice. After fruitless diplomatic exchanges the matter was referred to

119

the council of the League of Nations. The dispute was settled on May 28, 1933, when the Majlis ratified a new and much reduced concession which had been negotiated between the Company and the Persian Government.

Until about this time, except for American, French, and Dutch participation in Iraq Petroleum Company, Ltd., the oil production of the Middle East, chiefly in Persia with a small amount from Egypt, was by British companies. The Standard Oil Company of California about the end of 1928 acquired an oil concession covering most of the Sheikdom of Bahrein, a British protectorate. After considerable obstruction by the Colonial Office, clear title was secured August 1, 1930, and the discovery well of an important oil field was completed in June 1932. The Company, by agreement of May 29, 1933, also secured a concession over an extensive area in Saudi Arabia. A small oil well was completed in 1936, during which year a half interest in its Middle Eastern operations was sold to The Texas Company. Bahrein operations continued to be conducted by Bahrein Petroleum Company, Ltd., and those in Saudi Arabia by California Arabian Standard Oil Company. Drilling continued on the first prospect, the Damman dome, with but indifferent success until ten wells had been drilled. One of them was deepened and completed in the highly productive Arab zone in 1938 and in 1939 the area of the concession was substantially enlarged.

Meanwhile, Gulf Oil interests which had surrendered Bahrein as a result of the Red Line Agreement, had escaped its toils by selling their interest in Iraq Petroleum Company, Ltd. They tried for a concession over the Sheikdom of Kuwait, another British protectorate. Blocked for years by the Colonial Office, they finally joined with their chief competitor, Anglo-Iranian. Kuwait Oil Company, Ltd., was organized as a jointly owned company. Concession was secured December 23, 1934, and the discovery well of one of the greatest oil fields in the world was completed in February 1938.

Secretary of Interior Harold L. Ickes proposed in 1943 that the United States Government should purchase California Arabian Standard Oil Company, its properties or a share in them. Petroleum Reserves Corporation was organized as a vehicle for this operation and negotiations were carried on for several months but failed. Hardly had the reverberations of the domestic oil industry's vociferous objections to government in oil died away when the proposal was changed to one of building a government-owned pipe line across Arabia to the eastern Mediterranean and on February 6, 1944, the Secretary was able to announce agreement in principle between the Government and the companies.

World attention was focused on Middle Eastern oil again in the autumn of 1944 when a Soviet mission some 60 persons strong and headed by Sergi I. Kavtaradze, Vice Commissar for Foreign Affairs, appeared in Teheran and demanded reinstatement of the old Koshtaria concession of 1916 for the northern provinces. This concession had been canceled by the Russo-Persian Treaty of Friendship of February 16, 1921. The demand was refused. There followed the Soviet-managed separatist revolution of 1945 and 1946 in Soviet-occupied Azerbaijan and the northern provinces. In January 1946, Iran referred the dispute to the Security Council of United Nations. Direct negotiations between the parties to the dispute was authorized but nothing came of it. Occupation of Iranian territory by British, American, and Soviet troops had been sanctioned by a tripartite treaty which expired on March 2, 1946. British and American troops retired but Soviet troops remained and retired only after another protest to the Security Council and after the announcement by the Iranian government on April 5 of an agreement with the Soviet for a jointly owned company to explore and exploit the northern provinces, an agreement subject to ratification by the Majlis. There were further difficulties and increasing pressures but with the withdrawal of the Red army Iran was able to reoccupy and reëstablish its authority in the rebel areas. On October 22, 1947, the Majlis declared the proposed agreement of April 4, 1946 to be null and void and announced that Iran would embark on a five-year exploration program to be financed out of its own resources.

Meantime in spite of the agreement in principle for a United States owned Arabian pipe line, the domestic industry continued to object and it appeared doubtful whether the Government would go through with the project. The interested companies started surveys and purchase of rights-of-way and in 1945 Trans-Arabian Pipe Line Company (Tapco) was formed by them. In January 1947, its directors authorized construction of a 30–31-inch line with ultimate capacity of 330,000 barrels daily. In the summer of 1946, Standard Oil Company (New Jersey) and Socony-Vacuum Oil Company, Inc., entered into negotiations for the purchase of interests in Arabian American Oil Company (Aramco), as California Arabian Standard Oil Co. had come to be called. As of December 2, 1948, Jersey acquired a 30 per cent and Socony-Vacuum a 10 per cent interest in Aramco and in Tapco. Construction of the Tapco line has been delayed by difficulties in securing export licenses. The line is now operating.

At present there are at least four areas of tension in the Middle Eastern oil situation. The Soviet desire for expansion into northern Iran is still unsatisfied. The Supplemental Agreement to the Anglo-Iranian's 1933 Concession is still unratified by the Majlis and seems to have become something of a political football. Efforts are being made to renegotiate the Iraq concession. The Iraq government continues the blockade of Israel in so far as oil of Iraq origin is concerned. The blockade has existed since May 1948.

GEOGRAPHY AND GEOLOGY

The oil fields thus far discovered in the Middle East, except those of Egypt, lie in the flanks of the Persian Gulf geosyncline. This great trough contains a series of sedimentary rocks 50,000 to 60,000 feet thick at its deepest point. These rocks, which contain the oil deposits, dip almost imperceptibly away from the great complex of ancient crystalline and metamorphic rocks with younger volcanic rocks which, except for strips of coastal plain, outcrop along the shores of the Red Sea from southern Sinai to the Yemen. Its widest outcrop bulges northeastward to the Hail-Duwadini line and the deserts of the Lesser Nefud. The trough was formed by the southwestward and southern thrusting which formed the Alps-Himalaya mountain system, chiefly represented in Iran by the Zagros and in Turkey by the Taurus mountains. It is asymmetrical; the shorter flank with steeper folding being the outside or mountainward flank which occupies the Iranian coastal plain and passes through northeastern Iraq, northern Syria, and southern Turkey. The axis of the trough is in the Persian Gulf near the eastern shore which it roughly parallels. It crosses to the north in the valley of the Tigris River at a point about 75 miles north of Baghdad. To this point the strike of the axis is approximately northwest-southeast. From here it curves eastward to the crossing of the Syrian border. It turns to a strike of WSW–ENE as it passes through Syria thence to SW–NE or even nearly north-south in Israel and Sinai. The trough thus forms a great inverted V almost coinciding as to location with the "Fertile Crescent" of the historians.

The oil fields thus far developed lie on the flanks of the eastern horn of this great crescent-shaped trough; those of Saudi Arabia, Qatar, Bahrein, Kuwait, and southern Iraq on the inside or gently dipping flank; those of Iran, northern Iraq, and Turkey on the outside or mountainward flank. The less important oil fields of Egypt are within the Gulf of Suez graben or down dropped block and are on or within a few miles of the shore of the Gulf.

The oil-producing formation of Iran and northern Iraq is a transgressive limestone approximately one thousand feet thick known in Iran as the Asmari limestone and of Miocene age and at Kirkuk, Iraq, as the Main limestone and of Eocene age. The reservoir rock of the fields on the western or Arabian flank of the syncline are likewise of limestone, except for the true sands of the immense Burghan field of Kuwait and possibly the newly discovered fields in southern Iraq. These limestone reservoirs are of Jurassic and Cretaceous age.

Oil and gas seepages are of common occurrence in Iran and Iraq but notably of rare occurrence on the Arabian side where they have been found thus far only in Kuwait and Bahrein.

All of the twenty-three fields thus far discovered are included within an area 1100 miles long and striking NW–SE, the median line of which lies in the Persian Gulf and follows generally the Euphrates River. It is 1100 miles from the southernmost field, Ain Harad in Saudi Arabia, to the northernmost field, Ramandag in Turkey. It is approximately 800 miles from the southernmost field now in exploitation, Qatar or Abqaiq, to Kirkuk in Iraq. Kirkuk is the northernmost of the important fields and lies approximately 500 miles southwest across high mountain ranges and the deserts of the Iranian plateau from Baku, oil capital of the U. S. S. R.

The Iranian fields thus far developed are in the foothills of the Zagros Mountains and within 50 to 200 miles of the northeastern corner of the Persian Gulf. Similarly the Arabian fields are all within little more than 100 miles of the western shore of the Gulf.

In 1948 a well swabbing 300/400 of oil barrels daily was completed on the Ramandag anticline, southern Turkey. Production is from a 225-foot section of Cretaceous limestone, said to be dolomitic. A number of wells have been drilled but they do not flow and the field is not yet in production.

PRODUCTION

Production of oil in the Middle East has increased rapidly since the close of World War II as will be evident from the attached table. Currently (October 1950) it must be close to two million barrels daily. Production for the entire area averaged 1,829,000 barrels daily for August as compared with an average of approximately 1,440,000 barrels daily for the year 1949.

IRAQ, A CASE HISTORY

William Knox D'Arcy, an Englishman who had made a fortune from the Mount Morgan gold mine, in Queensland, in 1901 secured an oil concession covering the southwestern provinces of Persia. His earliest attempts to find oil were not successful and about 1907 or 1908 he sold an interest in his venture to Lord Strathcona and Burmah Oil Company, Ltd. On May 26, 1908, the discovery well in the Masjid-i-Suliaman field was completed. This was the discovery of commercial oil production for the Middle East.

D'Arcy sold his remaining interest to his partners and in 1909 the Anglo-Persian (now Anglo-Iranian) Oil Company, Ltd. was formed. Construction of a pipe line from the field and of a refinery at Abadan were commenced. The line was completed in 1911 and the refinery was in full working order by early 1914.

On May 29, 1914, the British Government bought a majority of the shares of the company under an agreement by which its commercial and financial affairs continue to be directed by its board, its

OIL PRODUCTION IN THE MIDDLE EAST

(Thousands of Barrels)

Year	Iran	Iraq	Bahrein	Saudi Arabia	Kuwait	Egypt	Total
1911						21	21
1912						214	214
1913	1,857					98	1,955
1914	2,010					753	3,663
1915	3,616					212	3,828
1916	4,477					404	4,881
1917	7,147					943	8,090
1918	8,623					1,935	10,558
1919	10,139					1,517	11,656
1920	12,230					1,042	13,272
1921	16,673					1,255	17,928
1922	22,247					1,188	23,435
1923	25,230					1,054	26,284
1924	32,373					1,122	33,495
1925	35,038					1,226	36,264
1926	35,842					1,188	37,030
1927	39,688	338				1,267	41,293
1928	43,461	713				1,842	46,016
1929	42,145	798				1,868	44,811
1930	45,833	909				1,996	48,738
1931	44,376	900				2,038	47,314
1932	49,471	836	1			1,895	52,203
1933	54,392	917	31			1,663	57,003
1934	57,851	7,689	285			1,546	67,371
1935	57,273	27,408	1,265			1,301	87,247
1936	62,718	30,406	4,654	20		1,278	99,076
1937	77,804	31,836	7,762	65		1,196	118,663
1938	78,372	32,643	8,298	495		1,581	121,389
1939	78,151	30,791	7,589	3,934		4,666	125,131
1940	66,317	24,225	7,074	5,365		6,505	109,486
1941	50,777	12,650	6,794	5,871		8,546	84,638
1942	72,256	19,726	6,241	4,530		8,275	111,028
1943	76,000	24,848	6,572	5,475		8,953	121,848
1944	102,045	30,993	6,714	7,794		9,416	156,962
1945	130,526	35,112	7,309	21,311		9,406	203,664
1946	146,819	35,665	8,010	59,944	5,931	9,070	265,439
1947	154,511	35,834	9,411	89,079	16,225	8,627	313,687
1948	190,395	26,115	10,915	142,853	46,098	13,398	429,774
1949	202,839	29,566	10,967	174,009	92,163	15,504	525,048
Totals ..	2,142,422	440,918	109,892	520,745	160,417	136,009	3,510,403

actions subject to veto by government directors "only in respect of matters of general policy, such as the supervision of the activities of the company as they may affect questions of foreign and military policy." This relationship has continued and seems to have worked remarkably well.

Shortly after securing the Persian grant, D'Arcy commenced negotiations for a concession in Mesopotamia, then a part of the Turkish Empire. The wily Turk kept the matter dangling. A concession was always about to be issued but it was never closed. On July 3, 1904, the German interests, the Anatolian Railway Company–Deutsche Bank group, secured permission to examine Mesopotamian oil prospects and a year's option for a 40-year oil concession. An imposing technical mission made the examination. Its report is said to have been moderately favorable to unfavorable and the option was not exercised. D'Arcy continued to try for a concession and, doubtless at the instigation of his representative, the Germans were informed that their option had expired. They countered with a claim for 20,000 pounds said to have been expended for geological and other work and, since the claim was not paid, they subsequently contended that their option was still in force.

Negotiations were resumed between the Turks and D'Arcy group in 1906 and continued during 1907. They were interrupted by the Young Turk revolution of 1908 but resumed in 1909. They were continued against a background of Turkish difficulties, domestic and international. About 1911, the Royal Dutch-Shell group came into the picture and in 1912 Turkish Petroleum Company, Ltd. was organized by Sir Ernest Cassel, an English banker of German birth. They became equal partners with the German group and the partnership acquired all of the German claims, good, bad, and indifferent. An effort was made to revive the Anatolian Railway grant of 1904. In 1913 the D'Arcy group nearly succeeded in securing the concession but was blocked by the German ambassador.

In October 1912, the Deutsche Bank, National Bank of Turkey, and Anglo-Saxon Petroleum Company, Ltd., then partners in Turkish Petroleum Company, Ltd., addressed to the Company the so-called self-denying letter reading in part "we will not directly or indirectly be interested in the production or manufacture of crude oil in the Turkish Empire in Europe and Asia apart from our interest in Turkish Petroleum Company, Ltd." The British and German governments got together in 1913 in an attempt to compromise the difficulties and conflicts of their subjects in an effort to secure the Mesopotamian concession. Representatives of the two governments and of the various claimants negotiated an agreement signed March 19, 1914, titled, *Arrangements for Fusion of Interests in Turkish Petroleum Concessions of the D'Arcy Group and of the Turkish Petroleum Company,* generally referred to as the *Foreign Office Agreement.* By this agreement all of the interests were fused into Turkish Petroleum Company, Ltd., of which the D'Arcy group got a 50 per cent interest, the Deutsche Bank and Royal Dutch-Shell groups got 25 per cent each, and provision was made for "a beneficiary five per cent interest without voting rights" for C. S. Gulbenkian, to be contributed equally by the D'Arcy group and the Royal Dutch-Shell group. Clause 10 of this agreement provides that the participating groups "shall give undertakings on their own behalf and on behalf of the companies associated with them not to be interested directly or indirectly in the production or manufacture of crude oil in the Ottoman Empire in Europe and Asia" with certain minor exceptions "otherwise than through the Turkish Petroleum Company." These agreements were apparently the bases for the famous "Red Line Agreement" signed by partners in Turkish Petroleum Company, Ltd., on July 31, 1928.

Actually, at this point the Turkish Petroleum Company owned no concessions; only claims. In consequence of the united front developed by the Foreign Office Agreement, however, the British and German ambassadors made representations to the Porte asking that oil concessions covering the vilayets of Mosul and Baghdad be granted to the company. The Grand Vezir on June 28, 1914 advised the ambassadors that his government "consents to lease the petroleum resources discovered and to be discovered in the vilayets of Mosul and Baghdad, reserving to itself the right to determine the amount of its participation as well as general conditions of the contract." There were further provisions which were vehemently protested by the ambassadors. As late as July 22 no agreement had been reached and the Turkish Government had asked that a representative of the Company come to Constantinople in order to settle the definitive terms of the concession.

World War I intervened a week later. During the war Britain enmeshed herself in a tangle of conflicting agreements with some of her allies regarding the dismemberment of the Ottoman Empire. Chief of these were the Sykes-Picot agreement with the French and that covered by the notes exchanged between Sir Henry McMahon and the Sharif of Mecca. At the outbreak of the war the Deutsche Bank interest was taken over by the British Custodian of Enemy Property and in December 1918 it was expropriated as enemy property. It was transferred to the French by the terms of the *San Remo Oil Agreement* of April 25, 1920, and is held by the Compagnie Française des Petroles.

The United States, not having declared war on Turkey, was not officially a party to efforts to make a peace. Britain received the equivalent of mandates over Mesopotamia and Palestine and France over Syria and the Lebanon at San Remo, in April 1920. The peace with Turkey was finally concluded at Lausanne, July 24, 1923.

The United States looked with disfavor upon the British-French partitioning of Mesopotamian oil. We were in one of our periodic scares that our oil resources were about exhausted. The argument, however, was pitched on broader grounds. We insisted upon principles agreed at Paris as set forth in Mandate "A." The more important of these briefly were "That there be guaranteed to the nationals or subjects of all nations treatment equal in law and fact to that accorded subjects of the Mandatory power" and "That no exclusive economic concessions covering the whole of any Mandated region or sufficiently large to be virtually exclusive shall be granted." In other words, the Open Door. Ambassador Davis submitted our position on these matters to the British Secretary of State for Foreign Affairs, Lord Curzon, on May 12, 1920, and called attention to its still unanswered note, with specific attention to the San Remo Oil Agreement on July 26. On August 11, Curzon's reply was received. It was not satisfactory, noting principally "that due consideration must be given to all rights legally acquired before the outbreak of hostilities." He noted that "certain rights were acquired in Palestine before the war by American citizens while British interests, such as Turkish Petroleum Company, claim similar rights either in Mesopotamia or in Palestine." This brought a tart reply from Secretary Colby, on November 20, 1920. The general arguments were repeated. Touching the heart of the matter, however, the Secretary observed "that such information as this Government has received indicates that, prior to the war, the Turkish Petroleum Company, to make specific reference, possessed in Mesopotamia no rights to petroleum concessions or to the exploitation of oil."

Curzon's next note was nicely timed. It was delivered to Ambassador Davis on the afternoon of March 2, 1921, when the Harding administration would succeed that of Wilson within a matter of hours. "I desire to make it plain that the whole of the oil fields (Mesopotamia) . . . are the subject of a concession granted before the war by the Turkish Government to the Turkish Petroleum Company." In this able note Curzon furthermore called attention to American inconsistencies with regard to the Open Door in Central America and the Caribbean as well as in the Philippines. Charles E. Hughes succeeded Colby as Secretary of State but the American position did not change and the Mesopotamian matter continued in dispute.

Early in 1921, Herbert Hoover, then Secretary of Commerce in the Harding cabinet, called a meeting of oil company representatives and urged that they expand their foreign producing operations. A result of this meeting was that a group of seven companies in early November addressed Secretary Hughes, stating that they desired to make petroleum investigations in Mesopotamia. Out of this group finally crystallized the American position in Mesopotamian oil.

Sir John Cadman, formerly director in charge of His Majesty's petroleum department and high in Anglo-Persian Oil Company, Ltd., made a professional visit to the United States in the early winter of 1921. Actually he seems to have come to suggest a solution of the vexing problem of Mesopotamian oil.

A representative of the American group, following a meeting on June 20, 1922, called at the State Department to inquire how it would stand if American and British interests could negotiate an agreement on Mesopotamia. The Department would not object (1) "providing that no reputable American company which is willing and ready to participate will be excluded by the agreement decided upon and (2) that the legal validity of the claims of the Turkish Petroleum Company will not be recognized except after an impartial and appropriate determination of the matter." At this point the Open Door of Mandate "A" seems suddenly to have shrunk to an Open Door for Americans. A representative of the American group proceeded immediately to London and in late July and early August negotiated with the Turkish Petroleum Company group. A basis for agreement was finally reached but much time was spent in searching for an Open Door formula which the Turkish Petroleum Company would accept and which would satisfy the State Department. An elaborate scheme was worked out which provided for the selection of certain specific blocks for development by Turkish Petroleum and the subleasing at auction, from time to time, of additional blocks—Turkish Petroleum not to be a bidder. Secretary Hughes agreed, with a number of "ifs," regarding which he seems to have been easily satisfied, that his Department would not consider the arrangement "contrary to the spirit of the Open Door policy."

Negotiations between the interested American companies and the partners in Turkish Petroleum continued over a number of years, being held up most of the time by C. S. Gulbenkian, one of the partners in Turkish Petroleum.

Notwithstanding the insistence of our State Department that the Grand Vezir's promise of 1914 was not a concession and therefore not valid, the claim of the Turkish Petroleum group, strongly supported by the British, was a cloud on title which effectively blocked any other disposition of the oil rights in Mesopotamia until the British-managed Kingdom of Iraq could be established by the promulgation of a constitution and crowning of the British nominee Faysal as its king on August 23, 1921, and after the extinguishment of Turkish title by the Lausanne Treaty. Finally the old claims were abandoned and the position of Turkish Petroleum rested squarely on a new concession signed March 14, 1925. The American group, by now potential participants, hailed this as "the first step toward possible development of oil in Mesopotamia." The State Department apparently was relieved to see so troublesome a question settled "so that presumably the present claims are based not on the prewar claims of Turkish Petroleum Company, but upon the recent alleged concessionary grant."

The Near East Development Corporation was incorporated February 3, 1928, to represent the American group; then consisting of Atlantic Refining Company, Gulf Oil Corporation of Pennsylvania, Pan American Petroleum and Transport Company, Standard Oil Company of New York and Standard Oil Company (New Jersey). The rights of all other partners have since been acquired by Standard Oil Company (New Jersey) and Socony-Vacuum Oil Company, Inc., successor to Standard Oil Company of New York.

The State Department was not particularly successful with its "Open Door" campaign. The concession of 1925, as has been noted, contained provision for the subleasing at auction of certain blocks of leasehold. I cannot find that any such blocks were ever so subleased. The concession was revised in March 1931, and Iraq Petroleum Company, Ltd., to which name that of Turkish Petroleum Company, Ltd. had been changed in June 1929, was given the sole right to exploit oil in the vilayets of Baghdad and Mosul east of the Tigris River. B. O. D. Company, Ltd., a German controlled British company, was registered March 1, 1928, and in May 1932 secured a concession of some 46,000 square miles, west of the Tigris, over lands which had been surrendered by I. P. C. Through a series of holding companies, Mosul Oil Fields, Ltd., and Mosul Holdings, Ltd., this concession apparently came into the ownership of Mosul Petroleum Company, Ltd., to which the name of Mosul Holdings, Ltd., had been changed, September 18, 1914, and which is a part of the I. P. C. group. A third company, Basrah Petroleum Company, Ltd., was registered by the I. P. C. Group,

July 22, 1938, and on November 13, 1938 it secured a concession over all of Iraq not otherwise covered. The I. P. C. group thus holds concessions over all of Iraq.

One of the problems of any foreign oil operation is that of maintaining friendship and mutual respect between the inhabitants of the country in which the operation is conducted and the skilled and technical employees, foreign to such country, who have to be imported to get the job done. There are basic differences between the foreigners and natives in language, in political and social viewpoints, and in religious beliefs. As important as any of these, however, is the unavoidable difference in economic status and consequent inequality in treatment of the two groups. The foreigners are skilled technicians and professional men who bring the "knowhow." They must be paid wages, generally in excess of those which they receive at home, and must be fed, housed, and generally cared for on a scale as good as or better than that to which they have been accustomed. Generally these foreigners are transients and this is particularly true for Americans. They do not become citizens of the country in which they work. They expect to save a stake and return home in a few years. Many of them do not even make a serious attempt to learn the language of the country, particularly. when the language appears to be as difficult as Arabic. The native workers, on the other hand, are generally unskilled and of low economic status even according to the standards of their own country. A few professional men, generally lawyers, with occasional doctors and engineers, make up the native position in the higher or middle salary brackets. The countries of the Middle East are poor countries and competition for jobs as unskilled or little skilled workers is such that the companies find themselves under no such compulsion to pamper their native labor as is the case with foreign employees.

I have described conditions which exist and which, it seems to me, must exist during the early years, the years of initiation of oil operations, in any country. If this and the collection of royalties and taxes by the government were all that çitizens of the producing country could look forward to the outlook would be far from rosy. Fortunately, such is not the case. Experience has taught companies operating in foreign fields that it is advantageous from all viewpoints to train citizens of the country to occupy as many of the skilled and higher jobs as possible. The field forces of the companies actually in production in the Middle East, according to recent reports, consist of approximately 130,000 men. Of these some 85 per cent are citizens of the country in which they are working. For Iran and Iraq where oil operations have been carried on for a long period and have reached, temporarily at least, a fairly stable state, 95 per cent of the field employees are citizens. For the other producing countries, Kuwait, Bahrein, Qatar, and Saudi Arabia, where oil operations are of much more recent origin and still in an expanding state, only 70 per cent of the field force are citizens of the country of operation. As the natives learn and become competent to carry on operations requiring skill they replace the foreign employees.

Consciousness of an obligation to their native employees, beyond the wage paid and minor benefits, has developed slowly and continues to develop with the companies. Among the earliest large-scale operations of British and American interests in foreign oil fields were those in Mexico from the early 1900's until expropriation in 1938. Unskilled labor—and it was truly unskilled—was merely paid a wage. In the worst cases of temporary employment men came down from the hills, brought a meager supply of food with them, worked a few days, slept in the brush, received their wage and went back to their homes. Skilled labor, almost altogether American drillers, their helpers, mechanics, and engineers, on the other hand, were properly housed, well fed, received medical attention, were paid a wager higher than at home, and generally received superior treatment. It was in a day when oil wells were flowed to full capacity or as nearly so as could be handled by transportation facilities. An oil field, except for its stripping stage, was regarded as likely to be of only a few years' duration. Except for directorships, the legal staff and occasional doctors and engineers, no Mexican citizens occupied an important position. Even the drillers and their helpers were foreigners. Venezuela and Iran became the next areas of large-scale operations; American and British in Venezuela and British alone in Iran. The Mexican mistakes were not repeated. The companies, largely through the camp system, became almost paternalistic and assumed responsibility for cultural and recreational needs as well. Creole Petroleum Corporation, the chief operating company in Venezuela, in 1949, for example, cites among the many activities with which it is associated, 9118 housing accommodations, 22 hospitals and dispensaries, 14 primary and 3 secondary schools, 25 sports and recreational clubs, 22 commissaries, 5 churches, and 19 playing fields; these for just under 21,000 employees. The Anglo-Iranian Oil Company in Iran employs more than half of those engaged in the oil industry in the Middle East, its field force of approximately a year ago comprising almost 75,000 persons. By the end of the war it had built over 10,000 houses for its employees and was providing houses, electric lights, water, and other facilities for some 16,500 of its workers including some 12,000 manual workers. It provides social welfare and recreational facilities as well as medical and other services for many of its employees. Its outstanding achievement, however, is in its far-flung educational program. It renders assistance to the government's Department of Education in the area where its main activities are located. It conducts classes and trade schools, including night schools, for workers, foremen, and clerks. It provides technical and commercial training in the company-built and operated Abadan Technical Institute and provides for the education and advanced training of selected Iranians in the schools and universities of the United Kingdom.

Obviously, in these advanced developments, the companies are performing duties which are proper functions of the state. It seems to me, that as oil operations become reasonably stabilized in any area, the state should assume responsibility for its normal functions and the companies should confine themselves as closely as possible to the oil business. Camps should exist only where necessary to take care of transient workers or in pioneer operations where normal living facilities are not otherwise available. Company efforts should be restricted to trade and industrial training, recreational facilities, medical services, supplementary provisions necessary to bring local facilities up to satisfactory standards, and such general attention as will tend to assure their workers of the availability of proper housing and opportunities for self-improvement.

I am advised that the Arabian American Oil Company plans to proceed somewhat along these lines through the establishment of towns, where necessary, or additions to existing towns, the building of proper houses and provision of necessary facilities. Through a building and loan operation it is intended that employees will be helped to purchase their own homes. The towns will be self-administered as is the case with any other municipality in Saudi Arabia.

The whole problem of company employee relationship, particularly in so far as it affects citizens of the nation in which operations are being conducted, is too big to be adequately discussed in these brief notes. I suggest, however, that the basic elements of the problem can be largely covered by four recommendations, as follows:

1. Field employees should consist, in so far as possible, of nationals of the state in which operations are being conducted.

2. Since ability and suitability should control the availability of the individual for any specific job or position and since equal work should receive the same pay, regardless of nationality, it follows that to achieve the ends expressed in the first recommendation, nationals should be trained to perform the work of the skilled and more highly paid jobs.

3. Permanent workers and their families must be properly housed, their health protected and they must be provided with adequate educational and recreational facilities. To the degree that the provision of these advantages is a function of the state, this responsibility should be assumed by the state. To the extent by which the state fails to do its duty, the companies must supplement or provide facilities. The essential point is that the worker should have these advantages, whether provided by the state, the companies or a combination of state and companies.

4. It is to the advantage of the state and of the company for the latter to confine itself strictly to its proper business of producing, transporting, refining and marketing oil. In a pioneer operation the company must engage in many additional activities in order to care properly for its employees but, as conditions stabilize, the state can advantageously assume functions now performed by the companies and the

companies can advantageously retire from the performance of such functions.

In closing I must apologize for my temerity in making some of these suggestions. One must be very conscious of the fact that while theorizing here as a self-anointed expert, some five thousand of our countrymen and a half dozen or so of our greatest companies are actually sweating over difficult problems in the deserts of Arabia with many more thousands of the peoples of that great land.

MAJID KHADDURI

The Scheme of Fertile Crescent Unity
A Study in Inter-Arab Relations

I. INTRODUCTION

The French historian Jacques Bainville once remarked that in order to build a federation, there must be a federating state. M. Bainville's statement might not be accepted by all students of politics, but it certainly reflects the state of mind that existed among the Arabs of the Fertile Crescent in their struggle to achieve unity and independence. "For a long while," says Musa al-Alami, "Arab thinkers have been hoping that an Arab Prussia would arise and unify us." [1] Whether in the form of an Arab Prussia or Piedmont, the Arab nationalists in the full hope of a Messianic expectation looked for the emergence of a strong Arab state that would unify the dismembered countries of the Fertile Crescent and eliminate foreign control. Of all the Arab countries, those of the Fertile Crescent, though relatively more advanced than others, were subjected to mandatory control. The nationalist movement, accordingly, had become very strong in this area, because its leaders had been able to arouse Arab national consciousness on the basis of opposition to Western imperialism. But it must also be remembered that the Arabs of the Fertile Crescent had attained a higher degree of social and cultural progress than the masses of the other Arab countries.

The hotbed of the Arab nationalist movement before and immediately after the first World War was in Syria; but the fall of the Arab Government of Damascus in 1920 and Faysal's accession to the throne of Iraq moved the center of Pan-Arabism from Damascus to Baghdad. From 1921 to 1941 Iraq became the most promising country to lead the Arabs toward the attainment of their national aspirations. At the outset, it is true, Iraq had to struggle for her own freedom from mandatory control; but when Iraq won her independence in 1932, a host of Arab nationalists from Syria and Palestine found safe refuge in Iraq and came to regard her as another Piedmont which would eventually achieve Arab unity. The Pan-Arabs argued that the existing regime in Iraq was an artificial creation of Great Britain designed to maintain her own interests and therefore unworthy of survival; the only truly Arab national regime would be that in which Iraq would form a part of a united Arab state.

The opportune moment for achieving this end, it was held, was in 1941, when Rashid Ali, supported by the Iraqi Army, raised a revolt against Great Britain. The Pan-Arabs sought—had Rashid Ali won the war—to liberate Syria from France, liquidate the Jewish National Home in Palestine, and create a united and independent Arab state in the Fertile Crescent. The Rashid Ali regime, which could not stand a thirty days' war, demonstrated not only the weakness of Arab power, but also the lack of understanding of their leaders, who, by turning against Britain, lost the support of a Power which, perhaps, would have been willing to help achieve the Pan-Arab ideal if the Arabs had sided with her against the Axis Powers. Viewed in retrospect, the Iraqi Army, instead of fighting Britain, might have taken the lead in driving out the Vichy forces from Syria and consolidated the Arab position in Palestine and thus would have greatly contributed towards the achievement of a Fertile Crescent unity. The shortsightedness of the Iraqi army officers was reflected in their desire to turn against a Power whose empire had already been on the move for freedom and to seek the support of another who had just embarked on a career of empire-building.

II. A GENERAL ARAB UNION VS. FERTILE CRESCENT UNITY

The collapse of the Rashid Ali regime was not ended without a lesson for both the Arabs and Great Britain, for it taught them to give concessions and accept a new compromise. On 29 May 1941, in the same day that Rashid Ali and his followers fled from Iraq, Mr. Eden, Secretary of State for Foreign Affairs, declared in his Mansion House speech that "His Majesty's Government will give their full support to any . . . scheme," that the Arabs desire for "a greater degree of unity than they now enjoy." [2] Such a scheme would not come into conflict with Great Britain's main interest in the Near East, and the Arabs, realizing the difficulty of achieving by arms their Pan-Arab dream, responded favorably to Great Britain's forward policy and began at once to give ready support to the democratic Powers.

Initial steps to achieve Fertile Crescent unity by negotiations with the British authorities in the Near East were taken up by Transjordan and Iraq. Amir (later King) Abdullah's negotiations emphasized mainly the unity of Geographical Syria (apart from the Fertile Crescent), while General Nuri of Iraq worked out a plan of Fertile Crescent unity in which Syria was to be included. Amir Abdullah's approach, which aroused little support among Arab circles, was discouraged by Britain; [3] while General Nuri's scheme, though sympathetically received, had to give way for the larger scheme of Arab unity. General Nuri submitted his plan in 1943 to R. G. Casey, Great Britain's Minister of State in the Near East, in which he advocated the establishment of an Arab League, comprising only the Fertile Crescent countries. The following is a summary of General Nuri's scheme: [4]

1. Syria, Lebanon, and Transjordan to be reunited to constitute one state.

2. The people of that State to decide its form of government, whether they have a monarchical or republican regime, or whether it be a unitary or federal state.

3. An Arab League to be formed; Iraq and Syria to join at once, the other Arab States to join if and when they desire.

4. The Arab League to have a permanent Council nominated by the member States and presided over by one of the rulers of the States, to be chosen in a manner acceptable to the States concerned.

5. The Arab Council to be responsible for: (a) defense, (b) foreign affairs, (c) currency, (d) communication, (e) customs, and (f) protection of minority rights.

6. The Jews in Palestine to have semiautonomy, and the rights to their own rural and urban district administration including schools,

health institutes, and police, subject to general supervision to the Syrian State and under international guarantee.

7. Jerusalem, a city to which members of all religions must have free access for pilgrimage and worship, to have a special commission composed of the three theocratic religions to ensure this result.

It is to be noted that General Nuri's proposals and Amir Abdullah's Syrian unity plan (later to be referred to as "Greater Syria") were not contradictory, but rather supplementary to each other; they aimed at forming some kind of union among the countries of the Fertile Crescent. Both of them were silent as to the future relations of Egypt and the Arab Peninsula to the Fertile Crescent Unity scheme, save the general provision in General Nuri's scheme that "other Arab States [may] join if and when they desire." [5]

The coming of Egypt into the sphere of Arab politics completely altered the nature of the scheme of Arab unity put forth by Iraq and Transjordan. Egypt, it is true, had followed in the past an independent course toward the achievement of her national aspirations, but the new circumstances of the last war made her realize the advantages if she led a bloc of several Arab states in the postwar period. But Egypt's leadership of the movement of Arab unity, which fortunately encouraged other Arab countries to join, such as Saudi Arabia and Yemen, had compromised the possibility of achieving a close and integrated union such as that contemplated by General Nuri. The Pact of the Arab League, as signed on 22 March 1945, had to be in the nature of a loose and confederal form in order to satisfy both local and dynastic interests.[6] But the Pact, in the meantime, made it possible, probably in deference to the aspirations of Fertile Crescent countries, for those "states of the Arab League that are desirous of establishing among themselves closer collaboration and stronger bonds than those provided in the present Pact" to conclude among themselves "whatever agreements they wish for their purpose" (Article 9). This permissible article, at least as it was later interpreted by Jordan and Iraq, became the basis for advocating such schemes as Greater Syria and the Fertile Crescent.

III. THE GREATER SYRIA CONTROVERSY:
FIRST PHASE

Amir Abdullah, who since 1920 had moved to Transjordan with the avowed intention of restoring Arab rule to Damascus, continued to cherish the restoration of Hashimi rule to Syria by advocating the unity of Syria and Transjordan into one country.[7] He declared war on Germany in 1939 and declared himself, in no uncertain terms, on the side of the democracies against the Axis Powers. In May 1941 he repudiated Rashid Ali's rise against Great Britain and took active part in opposing this movement. Upon the collapse of France in June 1940, with the consequential uncertainty as to the future position of Syria and Lebanon, Amir Abdullah revived his ambition of extending his control to Damascus.

In July 1940 Amir Abdullah sent two notes to His Majesty's Government expressing, *inter alia,* the aspirations of Syria and Transjordan to be reunited into one state.[8] The uncertainty of the military situation in the Near East and the sympathies of the extremists (Pan-Arabs) with the Axis Powers rendered Abdullah's proposals premature.[9] On 2 July 1941 Amir Abdullah communicated to His Majesty's Government a resolution passed by the Transjordan Council of Ministers on 1 July in which the Amir's Government requested the realization of Syrian unity in order to conform to its geographical unity.[10] While the reply of His Majesty's Government to Amir Abdullah (14 July 1941) emphasized that any movement towards further unity was entirely up to the Arabs themselves, it nevertheless discouraged any movement to be undertaken in the circumstances.[11]

When Oliver Lyttelton was appointed Minister of State in the Near East, Amir Abdullah sent him an invitation (11 July 1941) to visit Amman to discuss the question of Syrian unity. Mr. Lyttelton, while accepting the invitation, remarked that any movement toward unity ought not only to be undertaken by the Arabs themselves but also it should be undertaken under more favorable circumstances.[12]

When, on 13 September 1941, Mr. Lyttelton paid a visit to

Amman, friendly exchanges of views on Arab affairs were made. In discussing the situation in Syria and Transjordan Amir Abdullah made the observation that there was a noticeable instability and shifting of loyalties in Syria, while Transjordan proved to be more stable and loyal to the Allied cause. He pointed out, likewise, that Transjordan had contributed in eliminating Nazi influences in Iraq and Syria.. Transjordan, accordingly, added Amir Abdullah, should be given every opportunity and support to achieve full Syrian unity, namely, to reunite Syria, Lebanon, Palestine, and Transjordan into one state.[13]

While Amir Abdullah obviously obtained no positive help from Britain, he was nevertheless given assurances that his personal endeavors toward Syrian unity would not be obstructed.[14] He accordingly began to approach certain leading Syrian politicians in order to obtain their personal coöperation in achieving Syrian unity. He wrote a personal letter to Faris al-Khuri, a notable Christian Syrian nationalist well disposed to the Hashimi family, in which he pointed out that since Syria had been promised independence, it was therefore the opportune moment to reconsider the question of Syrian unity. Amir Abdullah stressed the motives which prompted him to write this letter on national rather than personal grounds, and pointed out that when Syrian unity was achieved, the form of her government would be entirely left for the Syrians to decide whether they wanted a monarchical or republican form of government.[15] Faris Bey, having consulted a number of leading Syrian nationalists, replied favorably to Amir Abdullah's letter; but he pointed out that a constitutional government should at first be restored before any movement to achieve Syrian unity is undertaken. Faris Bey declared that his Syrian friends were already in favor of the monarchical form of government and that the republican system was adopted only at a time when Syria was still under the French mandate. He assured the Amir that the Syrian nationalists were touched by the high motives which prompted him to consider the future of Syrian unity.[16] Amir Abdullah's earnest call, however, aroused no immediate action as Syria was then more preoccupied with the urgent problems of putting an end to the French mandate than with Syrian unity.

When the discussion at Alexandria (1944) was opened for laying the foundation of the Arab League, the question of Syrian unity was raised by the Transjordan delegate. Tawfiq Abu'l-Huda, Prime Minister and accredited representative of Transjordan, expressed his hope that "Greater Syria" could be achieved within the framework of the Arab League Pact.[17] The question was fully examined on 4 October 1944 when Prime Minister Abu'l-Huda suggested that both Syria and Transjordan should be given the opportunity to conduct separate negotiations for laying down a plan of unity before they would join the Arab League. Jamil Mardam, Syria's accredited representative, while he declared his approval in principle to the scheme of Syrian unity, showed dissatisfaction with Transjordan's approach to the problem. The accredited representative of Saudi Arabia, Shaykh Yusuf Yasin, inquired about the future form of government if Syrian unity were achieved. Jamil Mardam replied that Syria "was always in favor of a republican system." "Therefore," added Mardam, "Greater Syria could be achieved by the annexation of Transjordan to Syria as it had been a southern Syrian province under the Arab regime of Faysal." It was also stated that since the Palestine problem was pending solution, and Lebanon was opposed to joining, the scheme was not feasible in the circumstances and dismissed as premature.

Meanwhile the Greater Syria scheme was the subject of discussion both in the press and Arab political circles. Amir Abdullah made public his project by publishing the *Hashimi Book* (Amman, 1944) in which he stated his fundamental ideas on Syrian unity.[18] The project was sympathetically received by a number of Syrian nationalists, but it was severely criticized by leading Lebanese writers and politicians who argued that Lebanon accepted coöperation with the other Arab countries only on the understanding that her political independence and territorial integrity were respected. On 16 September 1944 the Maronite Patriarch Antun Aridha made a declaration to the effect that Lebanon would not submit to any scheme of union or unity, and demanded that a guarantee for her independence be given by France, Great Britain, the United States, and Russia. He earnestly stressed Lebanon's keen interest in establishing friendly relations with foreign countries, especially the

143

neighboring Arab countries, but was not prepared to accept any sort of tutelage whether it came from the West or the East.[19] Riyadh as-Sulh, Prime Minister of Lebanon, made declarations which stressed Lebanon's independence and stated that friendly coöperation between Christians and Moslems in Syria and Lebanon was more valuable to him than building an empire! [20]

Owing to this initial opposition both at the Alexandria Conference and in the press, Amir Abdullah postponed discussion of his scheme for the moment, only to open it again when the Arab League was formally set up in 1945. In the meantime he keenly felt the need for emancipating his country from the mandate and securing recognition for her independence before resuming his endeavors for achieving Syrian unity.

On 27 June 1945, the Transjordan Council of Ministers passed a resolution empowering its Prime Minister to request Great Britain to help Transjordan fulfill her national aspirations towards independence. The resolution was communicated to the British High Commissioner in Palestine who replied on 16 January 1946 that His Majesty's Government have decided to inform the United Nations, then meeting in London, of their intention to terminate the Transjordan Mandate. On 17 January 1946 Mr. Bevin, the British Foreign Secretary, declared in his speech at the Assembly of the United Nations that "regarding the future of Transjordan, it is the intention of His Majesty's Government in the United Kingdom to take steps in the near future for establishing the territory as a sovereign independent state and for recognizing its status as such." A Treaty of Alliance and Friendship between Great Britain and Transjordan was accordingly signed on 22 March 1946 by virtue of which Transjordan was recognized as an independent state. This Treaty, which was attacked by a number of Arab critics as inconsistent with the independence of Transjordan, was replaced by another signed on 15 March 1948.

Having attained independence for his country, Amir Abdullah proceeded to make certain constitutional changes in order to conform to the country's international status. On 14 May 1946 the Council of Ministers passed resolutions declaring Transjordan independent and its form of government monarchical and representative. On 25 May 1946 Amir Abdullah was formally proclaimed the first King of the Hashimi Kingdom of Transjordan (later renamed Jordan) in the presence of the country's notables and representatives of foreign countries. When, however, King Abdullah's Government made formal application for admission to the United Nations (26 June 1946), the application was (and has several times been) vetoed by the Soviet Union on the grounds that there were as yet no Soviet-Jordan diplomatic relations and "serious doubts" were raised about the country's independence. The question of admission to the United Nations, however, was not regarded as derogatory to Transjordan's independence and King Abdullah resumed his endeavors to achieve his Greater Syria scheme.

IV. THE GREATER SYRIA CONTROVERSY:
SECOND PHASE

Having achieved the independence of his country, King Abdullah began to contact a number of Syrian nationalists sympathetic to his scheme in order to induce them to influence the group in power to accept his project. He also tried to persuade a number of influential papers to initiate a campaign for his scheme as well as to raise the issue in the Council of the Arab League.

The Greater Syria scheme, as a principle of Transjordan's foreign policy, was formally announced by King Abdullah in his Speech from the Throne at the opening of Parliament on 11 November 1946. He pointed out that his primary interest was the security of "this western portion of Arab land" rather than personal or dynastic interest. In its reply to the Speech from the Throne, Parliament favorably reacted to the proposed policy of the King and approved it as the policy of the country.[21]

The formal announcement of King Abdullah's Greater Syria scheme as the official policy of his kingdom promptly aroused the opposition of both Syria and Lebanon and reopened the controversy in a more acute manner. Lebanon has been the more sensitive since the achievement of the scheme would destroy or encroach on her sovereignty. On 13 November 1946, Lebanon's Foreign Minister, Philip Taqla, and other leading politicians, denounced with angry clamors King Abdullah's policy as inconsistent with the policy which prompted Lebanon to join the Arab League, namely, respect of the independence of Lebanon within her present geographical boundries.[22]

The statement made by Lebanon's Foreign Minister induced a number of deputies in Transjordan's Parliament to raise the issue in the form of a question addressed to the Foreign Minister, Shurayqi Pasha, on 18 November 1946. Shurayqi made a detailed statement in reply to this question on 19 November 1946. He stated that while his country has been keen in observing the provisions of the Arab Pact, he would never be prepared to relinquish in any manner the duty of realizing the ideal of Syrian unity, not only because it is a matter that concerned one of the Syrian states (i.e., Transjordan), but also because failing to achieve that ideal would be inconsistent with Syria's natural rights and against her geographical and national backgrounds. He also hinted that it was not the business of Lebanon to interfere in this matter since Lebanon had long been recognized as an independent state and that the question of her joining Greater Syria would be entirely subject to the wishes of her people. As to the question of the internal form of government, the Foreign Minister added, the matter should not be regarded as an obstacle in the way of achieving national unity, since national unity was much more important than the form of government. He concluded that the future form of government for Greater Syria would be entirely left to the Syrian people themselves to decide.[23]

On 20 November 1946, when Lebanon's Foreign Minister, Philip Taqla, was still in Cairo as an accredited representative at the Council of the Arab League, he made several statements to local and foreign papers in which he reasserted Lebanon's opposition to the Greater Syria scheme. He pointed out that Lebanon and the other Arab countries joined the Arab League only on the understanding that each one of them was to respect the independence and existing boundaries of one another.[24] Shurayqi Pasha, Transjordan's Foreign Minister, who was also in Cairo representing his country at the Council of the Arab League, replied in the local papers, pointing out that Article 9 of the Arab Pact "permitted closer coöperation or union between one member state and another, and, therefore, it was entirely up to those people concerned to decide whether they wanted to join such a union, rather than to those enemies of the movement to express their views about it." [25]

Shurayqi Pasha's various declarations not only aroused Lebanon's apprehensions, but also incited a number of Syrian nationalists (mainly of the Nationalist bloc) who, in both Parliament and the press, reacted in the most violent terms against his outspoken claims to achieve Syrian unity. An avalanche of newspaper articles condemned King Abdullah and his Greater Syria plan as the work of foreign powers and therefore inconsistent with Arab national aspiration.[26]

On 23 November 1946, deputy Hamid al-Khoja raised the matter in the Syrian Parliament by addressing a question to its President and requested an official reply from the Government. Khoja's question induced a number of other members of the Syrian Parliament to discuss the problem of Syrian unity, and they repudiated Transjordan's claims and accused her ruler of furthering his own interests rather than the national interests of Syria. The main points of objection raised against King Abdullah's scheme may be summarized as follows: (1) the Anglo-Transjordan Treaty of 22 March 1946 subjected Transjordan to continuing British influence; (2) the Constitution of Transjordan which created a despotic government, left little freedom, if any, to the people; (3) the Greater Syria scheme might be used as a means to increase the influence of the Zionists; (4) the aspiration of Syria is to realize the larger scheme of Arab unity rather than the limited unity of geographical Syria.[27] In concluding the discussion, the Foreign Minister of Syria, Khalid al-Azam, gave the official attitude of his Government in the following statement:

From the very beginning of the Arab national movement, Syria has always striven hard to achieve the unity of the Arab countries . . . From the time when Transjordan was detached from Syria in 1920, following the tragedy of [French] occupation, Syria made many sacrifices for her freedom until finally she achieved her independence and sovereignty and was admitted to membership of the United Nations.

Syria, accordingly, has no desire to join a union which would encroach upon the attributes and rights enjoyed by other sovereign states, nor would she accept a constitutional system, which is contrary to her republican regime as was framed by her Constituent Assembly twenty years ago, and which she is still interested to maintain.[28]

In the meantime, a heated discussion on the Greater Syria scheme was made in the Lebanese Parliament on 26 November 1946. All the speakers denounced the project, and one of them went so far as to declare that if Transjordan continued to raise the issue she should withdraw from the League since all its members had agreed not to interfere in the internal affairs of one another.

While the Arab League had so far kept silent about the much discussed Greater Syria scheme, the issue was finally raised by Syria's Foreign Minister, Sa'dullah al-Jabiri, on 26 November 1946, with the following statement:

"Much controversy recently has been made about Greater Syria, and the press has discussed it fully while we [in the Arab League] —who should be more concerned about it—have kept silent. We [in Syria] repudiated the scheme from the very beginning, because we want to abide by the Arab Pact." [29]

The Foreign Minister of Lebanon endorsed the statement made by the Syrian Foreign Minister, but the Foreign Minister of Transjordan declared that his country was determined to realize Syrian unity because it had been the declared policy of Syria since 1920 (when the Syrian Congress passed a resolution to that effect, expressing the national aspirations of the Syrian people). Owing to disagreement among the accredited representatives, the question was referred to a committee, composed of the Foreign Ministers of the Arab States, for consideration. No final decision, it seems, was reached; but it was deemed necessary to declare that the Arab countries, in spite of this controversy, were quite keen about their solidarity within the Arab League. The following statement, signed by the Foreign Ministers of the Arab States, was made public on 28 November 1946:

There has been lately a discussion on the Greater Syria scheme which prompted the Foreign Ministers of the Arab States to hold a special meeting in order to discuss the question from its various angles. It has been decided, however, that no member state [of the Arab

_eague] has intended to encroach on the independence or sovereignty
_f another member state nor to interfere in its form of government.[30]

Meanwhile the Foreign Minister of Transjordan, immediately
_fter the meeting of the Arab Foreign Ministers, submitted a note
_o the Secretary-General of the Arab League in which the official
_osition of his country was reasserted. The text of the note follows:

The Government of Transjordan maintains that the calling for any
_nity or national union, through the proper political channels, without
_ncroaching upon any rights of others, should not be regarded a matter
_or disagreement. Since it is admitted that [the objective] of any Arab
_ountry is towards its geographical or national unity, it is, therefore,
_n the interests of any Arab country, whenever the circumstances for
_ts unity have become favorable, and without encroaching on any public
_r private rights, to put an end to that dismemberment, as it is incon-
_istent with the welfare and national aspirations of its people. In the
_pinion of the Government of Transjordan such an [action] will not
_e inconsistent with the independence of the States which are members
_f the Arab League, or with their existing forms of government, since
_he achievement of any union or unity would be decided by the people
_oncerned, where ultimate authority resides, in conformity with inter-
_ational obligations and the general [Arab] national consciousness.
While we appreciate the concern of the Committee of the Arab
_oreign Ministers in putting an end to the mischievous propaganda re-
_arding the Greater Syria scheme, as stated in their public statement;
[the Government of Transjordan], however, wants to reserve its
_oints of view because it is regarded as a national principle, based on
_ur own local interests and national program.[31]

The Joint declaration of the Arab Foreign Ministers (28 November 1946) failed to put an end to the Greater Syria controversy
since hardly had the ink dried when further exchanges were made
between the politicians of Damascus and Amman with accusations
and counteraccusations both in Parliament and the press. Resumption of further discussion was initiated by Transjordan when a question was raised in her Parliament which prompted Prime Minister
Ibrahim Hashim to reply, denouncing the existing regime in Syria
as an artificial creation of the abortive Sykes-Picot agreement,
while the establishment of Transjordan was "the fruit of the Arab
national revolt" and has ever since been a home for those Arab
nationalists who sought refuge in their times of trouble. Prime

Minister Hashim added that the present independent status of Syria was achieved only through the intervention of another foreign power (i.e., Great Britain) and that the evacuation might not be permanent unless Syria was reunited and thus became strong enough to offer sufficient resistance.[32]

This derogatory statement evoked bitter criticism in Syria and induced her Prime Minister, Khalid al-Azam, to reply in like manner. He pointed out that the present regime of Transjordan was not the fruit of the Arab national revolt, but the creation of Sir Herbert (later Viscount) Samuel, then Great Britain's High Commissioner in Palestine, who in a public statement made in 1920 declared the establishment of Transjordan following the tragic collapse of the Arab government in Damascus.

The devastating reply of Syria's Prime Minister naturally aroused the indignation of Transjordan, and her press accused the Syrian politicians of deliberately obstructing the achievement of Syria's national ideal. In Parliament, however, the Foreign Minister of Transjordan made a long but polite statement on 4 December 1946, in answer to a question in which he denounced the manner and substance of the statement made by Syria's Prime Minister. The Foreign Minister reiterated his Government's earnest efforts to achieve Syrian unity and appealed to the Syrians to realize their ideal by "uniting" the two portions of Syria, rather than by "annexing" the one to the other. The Foreign Minister's statement was approved by Parliament and a resolution was passed in which the Greater Syria scheme was confirmed as a national principle.[33] In the meantime King Abdullah continued to make statements to the effect that he would never cease his efforts to achieve Syrian unity. But such utterances, which hardly benefited his cause, roused the indignation of the Syrian nationalists.

On 15 September 1947, when Shukri al-Quwatli was reëlected President of Syria, the Greater Syria scheme was publicly denounced as inconsistent with Syria's national aspirations. President Quwatli went so far in his speech as to accuse King Abdullah of furthering his own personal ambition and then said, "if Transjordan really wants unity, let her people join the mother country [Syria] as a free republic." [34]

This damaging attack on King Abdullah, coming directly from Syria's President, marked the beginning of a shift in Abdullah's foreign policy. It was then hinted in Syria's political quarters that if ever unity was to be achieved with a neighboring country, such a unity should be made first with Iraq rather than with Abdullah's Transjordan.

V. THE IRAQI-TRANSJORDAN BLOC AND ITS RIVALRY WITH THE SAUDI-EGYPTIAN BLOC

Abdullah's failure to achieve his Greater Syria scheme prompted Iraq and Transjordan to reconsider their relations vis-à-vis the Arab League States. Iraq, in spite of certain local opposition, has, directly or indirectly, supported Transjordan's expansionist policy on the grounds that what benefits Transjordan today may benefit Iraq tomorrow. Opposition to Abdullah's policy has aroused Iraq's anger and induced the two Hashimi kingdoms to strengthen their position not only by cementing their relations by a formal treaty of alliance, but also by seeking support of a non-Arab power—Turkey.

Conversations between Iraq and Transjordan regarding the possibility of a federal union began early in 1946; but the scheme did not materialize owing to the opposition of a number of influential Iraqi politicians. The federal scheme was later modified to retain the separate identity of the two countries, but they would unify their military, cultural, and diplomatic affairs. Politically the two countries would establish a council, meeting alternately in Baghdad and Amman, composed of members appointed by each country to consider matters affecting both countries. Further, there would be a customs union and coöperation in all matters of common interests.[35] Even this scheme aroused criticism both abroad and inside the two Hashimi kingdoms. Syria and Lebanon showed apprehension lest it would be a step to enable King Abdullah to achieve his greater Syria plan. The most damaging criticism came from members of certain Iraqi influential quarters who did not approve of Transjordan's interference in Iraqi affairs and feared that such a union might be used as a means to support King Abdullah's expansionist policy.

Owing to such an opposition the scheme was reduced merely to a "Treaty of Alliance and Brotherhood," signed on 15 April 1947.[36] The Treaty provided for a close alliance and "eternal" brotherhood between Iraq and Transjordan and that both parties "consult with each other whenever circumstances demand fulfillment of the purposes intended by the preamble to the Treaty." The preamble stated that the security, coöperation, and complete mutual understanding on matters affecting the interests of the two countries were the purposes of the Treaty. In case of aggression by a third state, the two parties "must consult on the nature of the measures that must be used to unite their efforts to repel and ward off that aggression" (Article 5). The Treaty provided coöperation in unifying military techniques and training, and in diplomatic representation abroad. Article 6 permitted military intervention by one party to suppress disorder or a rebellion in the other. The Treaty, though it was criticized both in the Iraqi Parliament and the press, was approved and came into force on 10 June 1947.[37]

Transjordan's treaty with Turkey completed the series of three bipartite treaties between Turkey and Iraq (29 April 1946), Iraq and Transjordan (15 April 1947), and Turkey and Transjordan (11 January 1947). The initiative for signing a treaty between Turkey and Transjordan came from Turkey; but, as in the case of Iraq, it was welcomed by King Abdullah because it would enhance his prestige among the Arabs and help to strengthen the position of the Hashimi bloc in the Arab League against the Saudi-Egyptian bloc.

While the objective of Turkey, from her treaties with Iraq and Transjordan (to be followed by others with Syria and Egypt), was to complete a chain of treaties begun with Greece to meet the new balance of power in the Near East, it resulted in accentuating the division of the Arab countries between the Hashimi and the Saudi-Egyptian blocs and made it exceedingly difficult for Turkey to come to an agreement with Syria and Egypt. When General Nuri approached Syria early in 1946 to join such a Near Eastern pact he completely failed in his negotiations, because his scheme was suspected of being directed against the Arab League.[38]

The rivalry between the Hashimi and the Saudi-Egyptian blocs, aggravated by the opposition to an extension of Hashimi rule to Syria, resulted in a sharp disagreement on the question of Palestine. While the two camps could agree in principle that Palestine should be saved from Zionist designs, they could not agree on a working plan to save that country owing to their mutual distrust and rivalry. While a show of solidarity was maintained at the outset, disagreement on other issues was bound to affect the Arab stand on Palestine.

The show of solidarity among Arab rulers was initiated when President Truman proposed (31 August 1945) to Prime Minister Attlee to permit the entry of 100,000 Jewish refugees into Palestine. The Arabs protested against this proposal, because it contravened President Roosevelt's pledge to Ibn Sa'ud (15 April 1945) that no consideration of the Palestine problem would be made before consulting Arab leaders. President Truman's proposal prompted Mr. Attlee to suggest the reconsideration of the whole Jewish problem by a joint Anglo-American Committee of Inquiry before granting immediate entry for 100,000 Jews. The Committee, which endorsed President Truman's proposal, published its recommendations on 20 April 1946.[39] In order to cement Arab solidarity, Arab rulers were called to a meeting at Inshas (Egypt) by King Farouq on 28–29 May 1946 and in that memorable meeting the Arab rulers pledged coöperation in their opposition to Zionist claims to Palestine. A document, embodying certain recommendations to the Arab League for implementation, was solemnly signed by the six Arab rulers on 29 May 1946.

Prompted by the meeting of the six Arab rulers, the Arab League held an extraordinary session (8–12 June 1946) at Bludan, Syria, to discuss the implementation of the Inshas recommendations. The League decided to send two notes to Great Britain and the United States objecting to the recommendations of the Anglo-American Committee of Inquiry, and inviting Britain to discuss the future status of Palestine with the Arab States.[40] A secret resolution was adopted to the effect that if Britain and the United States failed to uphold Arab rights in Palestine, the Arab States will then reconsider their diplomatic and economic relations with these countries, including the cancellation of the oil concessions.

Arab solidarity was also maintained during the London Conference which met on 10 September 1946 to consider the future status of Palestine. The Arab Foreign Ministers, meeting in Alexandria on 12 August, decided that they would never accept any plan of partition or federation as a basis of discussion in the forthcoming conference. Owing to both Arab and Jewish refusal to accept a British compromise, Mr. Bevin announced in the House of Commons (18 February 1947) that His Majesty's Government had decided to refer the Palestine question to the United Nations General Assembly without recommendations.

To the outside World the Arab States continued to declare their full agreement on Palestine, while an avalanche of accusations and counteraccusations were exchanged between the two opposing blocs regarding the Greater Syria plan and the Turkish treaties. But such a false stand proved detrimental to the very cause they defended since it meant that the responsible Arab leaders pledged to their people something they could not fulfill owing to their conflicting views on other issues.

Arab solidarity on the Palestine problem was broken when Great Britain referred that question to the United Nations. While the Arab States tried to maintain an outward solidarity, the two Hashimi Kingdoms made reservations to the resolution passed by the Arab League Council (March 1947), in its approval to defend Arab rights in the United Nations.[41] Signs of this lack of solidarity were reflected in the opening speech (17 March 1947) made by the President of the League Council, Shaykh Yusuf al-Yasin, accredited representative of Saudi Arabia, who hinted that there were some who tried to "obstruct" the work of the League and he called them "the enemies of the Arabs!" On the other hand, the Prime Minister of Iraq, General Nuri as-Sa'id, disgusted with the policy of the anti-Hashimi bloc, called the two Houses of the Iraqi Parliament to a joint session on 24 March 1947 (when the Council of the Arab League was considering the Palestine question). A resolution was unanimously passed in which a firm stand was recommended on the question of Palestine. General Nuri, in his speech at this meeting (which reflected his hostility to the dominant bloc in the Arab League), went so far as to declare that if the League would not adopt a firm stand on Palestine, then "there no longer will be an Arab League." [42]

During the series of meetings of the Arab League, from the time when the partition resolution was passed by the United Nations (29 November 1947) to the acceptance of the first truce (11 June 1948), the disagreement was aggravated among the Arab States by such questions as the implementation of the secret Bludan resolutions, the question of Arab Military Command, and the acceptance of the truce. When hostilities were resumed on 18 July 1948 the lack of coöperation in the conduct of the war, controversies over the signing of the subsequent truce agreements, and Abdullah's claim to Palestine were facts which were no longer possible to conceal. To these initial differences between responsible Arab statesmen we should, indeed, ascribe the subsequent failure of the Arab States to win the Palestine war.

Had the Arabs won the war, there would still have been another war—military or diplomatic—to reach an agreement on the future of Palestine. King Abdullah, ever since Great Britain contemplated giving up the Palestine mandate, began to toy with the idea of uniting Palestine with Transjordan; but the opposition of the other Arab countries, with the possible exception of Iraq, forced Abdullah to agree to the Arab League resolution (April 1948) that Palestine, once saved from Jewish hands, would be handed over to "her people." When the Arab States failed to "save" Palestine, King Abdullah, regarding the resolutions of April 1948 no longer binding, began to revise his claims by demanding the annexation of Arab Palestine. While King Abdullah was making preparations for absorbing Arab Palestine, the events in Syria opened a new chapter of inter-Arab relations which had bearing on the larger scheme of Fertile Crescent unity.

VI. THE FIRST SYRIAN COUP D'ÉTAT AND THE OPENING
OF NEGOTIATIONS FOR A SYRO-IRAQI UNITY SCHEME

The failure of the Arab States to forestall the establishment of Israel demonstrated that parochial interests and dynastic differences were too strong to be ignored even in the face of a common danger. The Arab League, still young and incapable of conciliating differences, has merely served as a meeting place where these local forces were to clash. To some of its critics, The League has tended to promote rather than to conciliate conflicting differences.[43] Above all, the Palestine war has demonstrated that the Arab League could not afford security to the Arabs in the face of a new Israeli push. While the Iraqi and Transjordan armed forces were able to hold against the advance of the Israeli army, the Lebanese, Syrian, and Egyptian forces suffered defeat in a number of encounters.

The Arabs of the Fertile Crescent, aware that they were directly exposed to the danger of a renewed aggression, began once more to think in terms of a close regional unity within the framework of the Arab League. Since Abdullah's Greater Syria venture failed to command respect, it devolved upon Iraq to come to the fore to lead such a movement. But Iraq, probably trying to avoid Abdullah's mistakes, did not come out boldly for the scheme lest she would arouse the hostility of the anti-Hashimi bloc. Iraq accordingly began cautiously to watch events.

The opportune moment to open negotiations for a Syro-Iraqi unity offered itself on the morrow of the Syrian *coup d'état* of 30 March 1948 when Colonel Husni al-Za'yim marched on Damascus and seized power by force. The defeat of the Syrian army at the hands of the Israeli forces, it seems, was the immediate cause of the coup, though complaints of the corruptions and personal aggrandizements of the Quwatli regime had for long been the subject of accusations and counteraccusations of rival politicians.[44] Husni Za'yim aimed by his action at both ridding the country of a corrupt administration and starting a quick reorganization and strengthening of the national army. He regarded a close alliance with Iraq necessary to strengthen the position of Syria in the forthcoming truce negotiations with Israel and, if hostilities were ever renewed, Syria and Iraq would be able to resist any Israeli aggression.

On 1 April 1948, General Nuri as-Sa'id, Prime Minister of Iraq (who for long had played with the idea of a Fertile Crescent unity), sent Jamal Baban, the newly appointed Minister to Lebanon, to Damascus armed with a letter to Faris al-Khuri, then President of the Syrian Assembly. The letter expressed Iraq's "anxiety" and her "readiness" to offer any assistance that might be needed by Syria. Jamal Baban, who saw Colonel Husni al-Za'yim before Faris al-Khuri, offered Iraq's assistance and friendship to the new regime. Za'yim responded favorably to Iraq's friendly gesture, but refused to commit himself, when asked about the form of government, whether he would establish a republican or monarchical regime. When Jamal Baban saw Faris al-Khuri in the afternoon, the latter, while refusing to take part in any action, advised Iraq to coöperate with the new regime as the army officers were "friendly" towards Iraq.

On 3 April Amir Adil Arslan, then Za'yim's right-hand politician, informed the Iraqi Minister in Damascus that Syria was desirous of a unity with Iraq on the basis of a full autonomous status for each country. On 5 April the Iraqi Government replied that it would accept in principle such a scheme and would be ready to consider Syria's proposals if they were communicated through the proper legal channels. In the meantime, Iraq's suspicion that the intervention of a third party might disrupt negotiations, prompted the Iraqi Government to send a warning to Egypt to this effect. The Iraqi Government, however, hesitated to move quickly, probably either because it was afraid that the new regime might not last long, or because Iraq wanted the initiative to come from Syria. On 9 April Colonel Za'yim requested Iraq to conclude immediately a defensive military agreement and offered to send a delegation to Baghdad to begin negotiations. On 12 April the Iraqi Government responded by sending a military mission, led by Colonel Abdul Muttalib Amin, to discuss the Syrian proposals. Za'yim urged the immediate signing of a military agreement with Iraq because it would strengthen his position in the forthcoming Armistice negotiations with Israel.

The dispatch of the Iraqi military mission to Damascus aroused the suspicion of the Saudi-Egyptian bloc lest the *rapprochement* between Baghdad and Damascus would lead to the extension of Hashimi rule to Syria. Saudi Arabia and Egypt promised formal recognition and immediate financial support if Za'yim would maintain Syria's republican regime. Syrian delegations were accordingly sent to Riyadh and Cairo on 12 and 13 April 1949, which brought Za'yim assurances of recognition and financial aid. Not only had the Saudi-Egyptian intervention doomed a Syro-Iraqi dual monarchy, but also encouraged Za'yim to aspire to the highest position of his country—an ambition which sowed the seeds of disagreement between Za'yim and his army supporters who began to feel that this leader had betrayed the cause which prompted them to raise the revolt.

Iraq's slowness to respond to Za'yim's urgent call worked definitely to the advantage of the Saudi-Egyptian bloc. It was not until Iraq had received intelligence of the impending Saudi-Egyptian move to recognize Za'yim's regime that Iraq sent a telegram to Damascus inviting Za'yim to send a delegation to Baghdad to negotiate military and economic agreements. When the Syrian delegation submitted Za'yim's proposals to Iraq on 14 April, General Nuri, while he readily promised coöperation, pressed for a commitment, after a constitutional regime had been reëstablished, to a foreign policy consistent with Iraq's foreign policy. General Nuri made the observation that Syria had no definite foreign policy, and he wanted to know whether Syria was with the East or the West. "We," said General Nuri, "have a definite foreign policy, and we are in treaty relations with Great Britain." But Syria, continued General Nuri, has probably been "going with all and often against all." As to any impending Zionist threat, General Nuri assured the Syrian delegation that Iraq would immediately come to the help of Syria, without the need of a formal military alliance, since Iraq had always regarded a Zionist danger to Syria as a threat to Iraq too.

Events moved much faster to attract Syria to the Saudi-Egyptian side than Iraq had expected. The dispatch of a Syrian delegation to Cairo on 16 April and the visit of Azzam Pasha to Damascus on 18 April, resulted not only in committing Syria to the Saudi-Egyptian bloc, which was later cemented by Za'yim's flying visit to King Farouq on 21 April, but also caused Syria to take a hostile attitude toward the two neighboring Hashimi Kingdoms. When General Nuri sensed that Syria was gravitating to the anti-Hashimi bloc, he decided to negotiate directly with Za'yim. General Nuri arrived in Damascus on 16 April and told Za'yim that Iraq was ready to give Syria immediate military aid for her defense. If Syria wanted an over-all military coöperation, which was indeed the need of all the Arab countries, then he would like to know what the Syrian proposals were. Za'yim replied that since the Zionist threat had receded, Syria was no longer in need of an immediate military agreement. He stated that Syria had recently received some arms and that more were on the way. He added, however, that he would instruct Amir Adil Arslan to study the larger plan of future coöperation with Iraq.

General Nuri's failure in his mission resulted in immediate denunciations exchanged between Syria and the two neighboring Hashimi Kingdoms and the closing of Syria's frontiers on 26 April. Rumors were also circulated that an impending military clash of the Syrian forces was imminent in view of the massing of the Hashimi forces across Syria's borders. Thus the first real attempt since the war at a Syro-Iraqi *rapprochement* had passed owing to the slowness of the Iraqi Government to act quickly and the intervention of the Saudi-Egyptian bloc.

VII. THE SECOND SYRIAN COUP D'ÉTAT AND
THE RESUMPTION OF NEGOTIATIONS
FOR THE SYRO-IRAQI UNITY SCHEME

The Za'yim regime, which was hailed at the outset as the dawn of a new reform era in the modern history of Syria, could not fill the political vacuum created by the elimination of the previous regime, because Za'yim failed to coöperate with the leading political parties or groupings and sought only the support of the army. Feeling his position insecure at the beginning, Za'yim appealed to Iraq for coöperation. When assurances of support were lavishly offered by Egypt and Saudi Arabia, he suddenly turned against Iraq and showed unwarranted hostility to the Hashimi family. Greater uneasiness was created by Za'yim's growing relationship with France. Hatred to France was the one thing which all the Syrian nationalists could agree upon, and Za'yim's move to seek her coöperation meant the restoration of French influence from which the Syrians had for a quarter of a century struggled to be freed.[45]

159

Za'yim's leading political opponents, who were silenced by intimidation and the suppression of rival political activities, resorted to clandestine intrigue and held a number of secret meetings in which the idea of a union with Iraq was broached. It was then proposed that a Syrian Provisional Government might be established near the Iraqi frontiers and which, by collaboration with the Iraqi Government, would overthrow the Za'yim regime.[46] Before these politicians had time to proceed with any seriousness, the Za'yim regime was tottering from within by lack of solidarity among the army officers to whom Za'yim owed his elevation to power. Petty jealousies and self-adoration started the rift between the leader and his army supporters, and Za'yim's pro-French policy and his quarrel with the two Hashimi kingdoms supplied adequate reasons for condemning him for "high treason" by a court martial; he was immediately shot. The leader of the second coup, Colonel Sami al-Hinnawi, assuring the nation that he was not seeking power, handed over authority to the leading Syrian politicians on the same day in which he liquidated Za'yim (14 August 1949). A Provisional Government was formed with Hashim al-Atasi, one of the most generally respected and disinterestedly honest politicians, at its head. But it was tacitly understood that the Military, in spite of their self-abnegation of power, could intervene at any moment if the policy of the government ran counter to their desires.

The second Syrian coup afforded Iraq another opportunity to resume negotiations for unity with Syria. While the official negotiations were conducted just as secretly as during the first coup, the scheme of unity had inevitably become the subject of discussion in the press as well as by public men and business groups in Iraq and Syria. Both the Syrian National Party and the Iraq Istiqlal (Independence) Party took active part in arousing popular interest in their countries. The People's Party, organized in August 1948 as an opposition party to the Quwatli regime, had already declared itself in favor of an intimate Arab unity among the countries directly exposed to the Zionist threat.[47] Further, there were many independent politicians, led by Hasan al-Hakim, who openly declared their ready approval of a Syro-Iraqi unity. Hasan al-Hakim went so far as to demand the immediate unity of Syria with

Iraq and Transjordan.[48] Finally, a number of leading army officers, including Sami al-Hinnawi, have been persuaded to accept unity with Iraq. Hinnawi's brother-in-law, As'ad Tallas, Undersecretary for Foreign Affairs, who took active part in the negotiations between Iraq and Syria, seems to have influenced the Army through his connections with Sami al-Hinnawi.

When the Regent of Iraq, Amir Abdul-Ilah, paid a visit to Damascus (5 October 1949), on his way back to Baghdad, he was welcomed at the Damascus Airport by Premier Hashim al-Atasi and the members of his cabinet. Among the guests were Sami al-Hinnawi, Commander-in-Chief of the Army, Faris al-Khuri, former President of the Syrian Assembly, and Sabri al-Asali, Secretary-General of the National Party, who recently had advocated unity with Iraq. The Regent made no public statement, but his visit and his private conversations with the Syrian leaders were gestures designed to test public opinion in Syria regarding unity with Iraq.

While private conversations between the Iraqi representatives and the Syrian leaders were all friendly and indicated agreement on the basic issues, no official commitment was made by the Syrian Cabinet. The Provisional Government of Hashim al-Atasi discussed the subject of unity during several cabinet meetings, but no final decision was taken as it was thought that so important a matter should be decided by the Constituent Assembly, representing the wishes of the people, rather than by a provisional government. Furthermore, while the majority of the cabinet wanted unity with Iraq, there were differences of opinion as to what sort of unity should be achieved. Some of the members of the cabinet insisted that Syrian independence and the republican regime should be maintained within the larger frame of the Syro-Iraqi union. Others demanded that both the Syrian Army and Syria's foreign policy should remain independent of the Iraqi Army and Iraqi foreign policy. But all accepted, if unity were ever achieved, that a Supreme Council of the Union should be set up composed of equal representatives of Syrians and Iraqis, presided over alternately by a representative of each country.[49] The Iraqi Government offered to accept the maintenance of the independence and the republican regime of Syria, but demanded that the Supreme Council be presided over by a single head jointly elected by the Syrian and Iraqi peoples. Iraq demanded, likewise, the formation of a Union Cabinet composed of a Prime Minister, and Ministers for Foreign Affairs, Defense, Finance, and Economics. Iraq and Syria were to be equally represented in this cabinet, which was to be responsible to the Union Council. Common affairs of the two countries were to be administered by the Union Cabinet and Administration, including diplomatic representation, a customs and monetary union, and the merging of the two armies under a unified command.[50]

The advocates of Pan-Arabism, who for long cherished the idea of an Arab empire, regarded the Syro-Iraqi unity plan but a step to achieve the larger scheme of Arab unity. They realized the local difficulties they would encounter, but they hopefully counted on the results of the forthcoming elections for the Constituent Assembly which was to decide on the question of unity with Iraq. Both the advocates of unity and its opponents appealed to the electorate for a final decision. The elections, which were completed in mid-November 1949, were carried out with relative freedom,[51] but the advocates of unity with Iraq, especially the People's Party, did not achieve any such spectacular gain as had been expected. "The elections," as they have been commented upon rightly, "have been characterized by public indifference."[52] Only a small percentage of the eligible voters went to the polls, including the women, who cast their ballots for the first time in an Arab country.[53]

The Constituent Assembly met on 12 December 1949 and elected Rushdi al-Kikhyah, leader of the People's Party, President of the Assembly. Speeches were made by Kikhyah, Premier Atasi, and others in which tribute was paid to the army and General Hinnawi, and declarations in favor of drafting a constitution on the basis of democracy and Pan-Arabism were reiterated.[54] In the third sitting of the Assembly (14 December 1949) Hashim al-Atasi was elected a temporary Head of the State to hold special legislative and executive powers until the Constitution should be promulgated.[55]

When discussion on the oath to be taken by the Head of the State was opened in the fourth sitting of the Assembly (17 December 1949), the questions of the future form of the Syrian Government and of Arab unity (i.e., unity with Iraq) were raised and there was much divergence of opinion. The opponents to unity with Iraq, under disguise of maintaining the republican regime for Syria, criticized the text of the oath for mentioning only Arab unity but omitting reference to the republican form of government. Akram al-Hawrani and Mustafa al-Suba'i, advocating the republican form, strongly criticized the text, while Abdul-Wahhab Hawmad argued that a reference to Arab unity in the oath was an anticipation to what the Constituent Assembly might approve or reject.[56] These opponents to Arab unity formed a bloc in the Assembly, led by Akram Hawrani and Abdul Baqi Nizam ad-Din, called the Republican Bloc. The advocates of unity with Iraq, such as Munir al-Ajlani and Zaki al-Khatib, strongly argued against any reference in the oath to the form of government, since they maintained that the form of government was pending discussion by the Constituent Assembly.[57] As these members, comprising the People's Party and a number of Independents, formed a majority in the Assembly, the text of the oath was accepted without reference to the form of government.[58]

The discussion on the text of the oath and the omission of any reference to the republican form of government had its repercussions in the Syrian political circles and in the army. Agitation outside the Assembly against unity with Iraq was aroused by the Republican Bloc and the Ba'th Party, but the deciding factor in this discourse, as indeed in all other major political decisions, rested with the army. General Hinnawi, it will be recalled, had definitely supported the move for unity with Iraq and, with the majority of the members of the Assembly supporting this move, it seemed that the question of unity with Iraq was a matter of days. But this very fact alarmed the Republican Bloc and their followers who could see no escape from this impasse save by winning the army to their side. Secret contacts were made between Republican leaders and a number of army officers, who, though having coöperated with Hinnawi to get rid of Za'yim, did not see eye-to-eye the policy of unity with Iraq as advocated by Hinnawi. The leader of this secret move was Colonel Abib al-Shishakli who, in the same way as Hinnawi had raised an army coup against Za'yim, now made a similar move against Hinnawi on 19 December 1949. Thus, the whole army, under a new command, changed its stand on the question of unity with Iraq. General Hinnawi, accused of "high treason" because he was seeking a "conspiracy" with a foreign power against the interest of his country, was arrested and sent to prison to await trial by a court martial.

When the Constituent Assembly met on 22 December 1949 Hashim al-Atasi, who was expected to be present in the Assembly to take the oath, failed to appear. It was quite clear to the Assembly that an important change in policy was expected, but one of the members cynically inquired whether the absence of al-Atasi, as it was announced in the Assembly on 19 December, was still for medical reasons.[59] Sa'id Haydar, an advocate of unity with Iraq, daringly asked whether authority resided in the Assembly or "elsewhere." If it resided in the Assembly, then it was the duty of the Assembly to discuss the "conspiracy" ascribed to those persons who took part in it. It was only a few days ago, said Haydar, that tribute was paid by this Assembly to persons who saved the honor of this country, but now we hear that these same persons have been arrested on the ground that they have conspired against the safety of the country and the army. "I demand," concluded Haydar, "that this subject be discussed in the Assembly to know who is really conspiring against the safety of the country."[60] The President of the Assembly replied that the question would be postponed until a new government was formed, since President Atasi had been unable to persuade anyone to form a cabinet owing to the present circumstances. Haydar's question, even after a government had been formed, was not answered until two months later when a heated argument was opened between the Republican Bloc, who had by this time seized power, and their opponents.[61]

The immediate problem which faced the Provisional Government after this new move was the proposed amendment of the oath put forth by Shishakli and the Republican Bloc. A constitutional problem arose since the text of the oath had already been accepted by the Assembly and any change made, even by the approval of the Assembly, would be construed as having been done under pressure of the army. President Hashim al-Atasi threatened to resign if the military continued its interference, but the problem was resolved by leaving the text as it was since the general reference to Arab unity was not construed to refer necessarily to Iraq but to all the Arab countries. Another problem arose as to who would form a government. President Atasi invited Nazim al-Qudsi, representing the People's Party, the largest single political grouping in the Assembly, to form a government; but Qudsi, who accepted the invitation on 24 December 1949, resigned on the following day as he resented the interference of the military in the formation of his cabinet.[62]

The cabinet crisis passed when President Atasi invited Khalid al-Azam (a former Prime Minister under the Quwatli regime) to form a government on 27 December 1949. Khalid al-Azam sought the coöperation of both the Republican Bloc and the People's Party, but it was understood that the ministers were not officially representing their parties.

When the Constituent Assembly met on 29 December 1949 the Azam government was requested to submit its program before a vote of confidence could be given. On 4 January 1950, Khalid al-Azam made a statement in the Assembly in which he stated, *inter alia,* that his cabinet would defend the independence of Syria and assert the republican and democratic form of government. He also stated the acceptance by his government of the Collective Security Pact which was then under negotiations in Cairo by the Arab League.[63] In the following meeting of the Assembly (7 January) the question of confidence in the government was discussed and the Prime Minister was criticized for asserting the republican regime but forgetting all about "Arab unity." In answering his critics, Azam replied that although Arab unity was his long cherished hope, he resented finding Syria like a "commodity" offered for sale by contending parties.[64] In spite of criticism a vote of confidence was given by the majority of the Assembly which only a few days before had asserted itself on the question of the oath, refusing to commit itself to a republican regime.

While it must be admitted at the outset that the initiative for change in the attitude of Syria toward unity with Iraq came from within, it is also true that the opponents to unity with Iraq knew beforehand how welcome such a move would be to the Saudi-Egyptian bloc and that they could count on both the material and diplomatic support of this bloc. No sooner had Shishakli completed his coup in Damascus than he headed a military mission to Cairo (8 January 1950) where he was favorably received by the Egyptian Government. He made a statement in which he stressed Syria's friendly attitude toward Egypt, his Government's support for general Arab collective security, and Syria's need for an Egyptian military mission.[65] From Cairo, Shishakli proceeded to Riyadh (12 January 1950) to repair the Saudi friendship which had been recently disrupted by Hinnawi's move to tie Syria with Iraq. The Shishakli mission was followed by the visit of the Minister of National Economy, Ma'ruf al-Dawalibi, to Cairo and Riyadh during February 1950, which resulted, after conversations with Egypt, in promoting commercial relations between Syria and Egypt, and after conversations with Riyadh, in signing both a loan and commercial agreements. The loan agreement provided that Saudi Arbia would supply six million dollars during seven months from the date of ratification of the agreement in exchange for Syrian commodities which Saudi Arabia would buy during the years 1955 to 1958.[66] These two agreements were immediately approved by the Syrian Constituent Assembly in its meeting on 11 February 1950.[67] While Munir al-Ajlani, an advocate of unity with Iraq, welcomed the signing of the agreements, he hoped that they would not be construed to mean that Syria would change her attitude towards other Arab countries such as Iraq. Husni al-Birazi cynically remarked that in his opinion the agreements require "thanks" to the lender and "pity" to the borrower.[68] But it has become clear that, in spite of the lip service paid to Iraqi unity and Arab coöperation, Syria has gone over once more to the Saudi-Egyptian bloc by Egyptian diplomatic support and Saudi money. The Egyptian proposal of an Arab collective security pact, to be signed by all the Arab League states in order to protect them from Zionist danger, was in fact designed to disrupt the Syro-Iraqi unity scheme which was advocated by Syrians who sought security from Zionism through such unity. Saudi Arabia, though the most autocratic monarchy in the Arab World, helped to reëstablish the republican regime in Syria, fearing the extension of Hashimi rule to Damascus. While the reactions of the official quarters in Iraq were outwardly calm, the advocates of Pan-Arabism were gravely disappointed and did not conceal their apprehensions regarding the recurrence of military coups and the intervention of Egypt to prevent the fulfillment of Arab national aspirations. Failing to achieve for the second time his plan of Syro-Iraqi unity, the Prime Minister of Iraq, General Nuri as-Sa'id, who had become the target of attack by the Egyptian press, resigned in order to ease the tense relations between Iraq and Egypt on the questions of Syrian unity with Iraq. Ali Jawdat formed a new government in January 1950 with Muzahim al-Pachachi, a former Prime Minister friendly to Egypt, as Foreign Minister. Pachachi, who was instructed to conciliate Egypt, visited Cairo late in January 1950 and arrived at an agreement quickly with Nahhas Pasha, Prime Minister of Egypt, that both Iraq and Egypt would abstain from any interference in Syrian affairs for five years after the ratification of the agreement. When the news of the agreement reached Baghdad, Pachachi was severely attacked for giving up Iraqi rights to negotiate with Syria in order to please Egypt.[69] On his return to Baghdad Pachachi held a press conference on 9 February 1950 in which he tried to justify his position on the grounds that his agreement with Egypt did not deny Iraq and Syria the right to unite, but that since the internal affairs of Syria were very unstable, it was only right that Syria must be left alone for a period of five years until a stable constitutional regime has been reëstablished.[70] The Pachachi agreement was repudiated, which reflected Iraq's anger with Egypt's intervention in Syria, and the Ali Jawdat government resigned in February 1950. Relations remained tense between Egypt and Iraq, though the new Prime Minister, Tawfiq al-Suwaydi, tried to ease the situation by a visit to Egypt during the meetings of the Arab League in March 1950.

VIII. THE GREATER SYRIA PLAN: FINAL PHASE—
THE ANNEXATION OF ARAB PALESTINE BY JORDAN

King Abdullah's failure to extend his rule to Damascus has not discouraged him from continuing his endeavors to achieve the

Greater Syria plan from a different direction. From the time when Great Britain contemplated giving up the Palestine mandate, it will be recalled, King Abdullah began to toy with the idea of uniting the lands on the two sides of the River Jordan into one country as part of his larger Greater Syria plan. The insistence of the Saudi-Egyptian bloc, however, led the Arab League in April 1948 to pass a resolution to the effect that the intervention of the Arab states in Palestine was not aimed at the territorial aggrandizement of any one of them, but merely to save Palestine from Zionism and handing over the country to "her people."

The failure of the Arab states to "save" Palestine offered King Abdullah an excuse for coveting the absorption of what remained of Palestine outside Israel. Since Syria and Lebanon had been pushed back to their frontiers and had signed armistice agreements with Israel, and the Iraqi forces had voluntarily evacuated the area under their control in favor of Transjordan, only Egypt and Transjordan of the Arab League states remained in *de facto* occupation of Arab Palestine. In the circumstances, the Arab League was faced with a new situation which required either the implementation of the resolution of April 1948, or the formulation of a new plan for Arab Palestine. Refusing to recognize any changes, though some of the Arab states made unofficial declarations in favor of accepting the Partition Resolution of 29 November 1947, the Arab League regarded the resolution of April 1948 as still binding and demanded the handing over of occupied Palestine to an Arab Government of "all Palestine." On 20 September 1948, an Arab Government was proclaimed with temporary headquarters at Gaza. Its cabinet, formed by Ahmad Hilmi Pasha on 22 September, notified the Secretary-General of the Arab League of its decision to regard "all Palestine" an independent state. Haj Amin al-Husayni, ex-Mufti of Jerusalem, arriving at Gaza on 28 September, entering Palestine for the first time after eleven years, was elected President of the Palestine National Assembly (1 October 1948). The Gaza Government was recognized by Egypt and Iraq on 12 October, and by Syria and Lebanon on 14 October.

The establishment of the Gaza Government aroused the resentment of King Abdullah and prompted him to proceed with his plan of absorbing Arab Palestine. He at first objected to the establishment of an Arab Government in Palestine and demanded its dissolution on 5 October. Attempts to bring the Mufti and King Abdullah to agree on a plan failed and Abdullah declared that he would bar the Gaza Government from territory controlled by his army. He appointed an Arab Legion Commander, Colonel Abdullah al-Tal, as military governor of Jerusalem, succeeding Ahmad Hilmi Pasha (who had become the Prime Minister of the Gaza Government), but abolished this position on 6 December.

A Palestine Arab Congress, claiming to represent all Arabs of Palestine, met at Jericho (1 December 1948) and passed a resolution declaring King Abdullah "King of Palestine." This inspired resolution was made to counteract the action of the Gaza Government and to prepare the way for the final annexation of Arab Palestine by Transjordan. On 20 December King Abdullah announced that he had appointed a new mufti of Jerusalem, Shaykh Hasam ad-Din Jarallah, former Chief Justice of the Islamic religious courts of Palestine, in defiance of Haj Amin Husayni's claim to the position. On 17 March, King Abdullah replaced the military administration of Palestine by a civil administration and the country became to all intents and purposes a part of Transjordan. In April 1949 the official name of Transjordan was declared to be the Hashimi Kingdom of Jordan, to be effective from the end of 1949. On 2 May 1949, the Jordan cabinet was replaced by another in which three Arabs of Palestine were included.

The official proclamation of the annexation, however, was not made until a few months later. King Abdullah, in consultation with a number of Palestine leaders, made preparations for new elections (20 April 1950) in which Arab Palestine was to return twenty deputies (i.e., half the membership of the Jordan Parliament). The new Parliament met on 24 April and passed a resolution approving the uniting of the area lying on both sides of the River Jordan into one country.

Jordan's action, while it secured the protection of Great Britain since her treaty with Abdullah would require her protection of the country within the new boundaries if it were the subject of aggression by a foreign power, aroused the resentment of the Arab

League. The question of annexation was raised in the Political Committee of the Arab League and it was decided, pending action by the League Council, that Jordan had violated the League resolution of April 1948. Expulsion from the League requires unanimity in vote, but even if Iraq were forcibly pushed into agreement (which appears doubtful), the action would merely accentuate the schism among the Arab League states, and would encourage Jordan, which has been suspected of negotiating secretly with Israel, to come to terms with that country.

IX. CONCLUSION

In reviewing the foregoing controversies regarding the plans put forth for achieving full or partial unity of the Fertile Crescent, the first important question to ask is: If the Arabs really want unity what is preventing them from achieving it?

A quarter of a century ago, when the Fertile Crescent had just been emancipated from Ottoman rule, no Arab thinker would ever question the feasibility of creating an Arab union comprising that area. When unity and independence were not achieved after the first World War, the Arab nationalists naturally contended that European imperialism had deliberately followed a policy of *divide et impera* since it was easier to dominate that area by creating several weak states than to allow it to unite, and hence to become difficult to control.[71] The Arab nationalists argue that since the Arabs were bound by a community of interests and aspirations—geography, history, and culture—they were, therefore, entitled to form a union.[72] They have, it is true, admitted that there were certain factors which run counter to unity, such as the existence of racial and religious minorities, variations in economic and cultural levels, and parochial indifference, but the rising tide of national feeling, accentuated by European control, was so overwhelming that Arab thinkers overlooked the disruptive local factors which might rise once European influence receded from Arab lands.

When the opportune moment to achieve unity had come (during the deliberations for setting up the Arab League in 1944–45), it was shockingly found that a number of Arab leaders were not only unprepared to accept federal union, but others were even reluctant to join any form of unity. Plans for uniting parts or the whole of the Fertile Crescent, it will be recalled, were not wanting; but the local forces that were working against them made it exceedingly difficult to achieve any one plan, in the circumstances. The question that may be asked then is how permanent were these forces and would it be possible to achieve Fertile Crescent unity under more favorable circumstances? Let us examine more closely the objections that have been put forth against each of the foregoing schemes.

To begin with, let us take the Greater Syria Plan. It may be said at the outset that both Syria and Jordan were agreed, in principle, on "Syrian unity"; but, it seems, they radically disagreed on the form and procedure of achieving that unity. First, it has been argued that the present treaty obligations of Jordan, as defined by her treaty with Great Britain, would be binding on the future state of Greater Syria if Jordan and Syria were completely united. The Syrians, it will be recalled, have strongly objected against being bound by a treaty with France which would encroach on their sovereignty. Unity with Jordan, it is contended, would be none other than replacement of French influence by British in Syria. The Syrian and Egyptian press have gone so far as to argue that Great Britain, seeking to extend her influence to Damascus, has encouraged King Abdullah to advocate unity.[73] It is also pointed out that the *rapprochement* between Turkey, Iraq, and Jordan, which Great Britain might have encouraged, is repugnant to the Syrians, because Turkey had annexed Alexandretta, without Syria's approval, by direct negotiations with France.[74] The argument that King Abdullah has been induced by Great Britain to advocate Greater Syria seems to be unjustifiable in the light of Abdullah's correspondence with Britain on that scheme.[75] In view of the strong opposition of Lebanon and Syria, might it not be also true that Abdullah has been restrained by Britain from pushing his plan against Arab opposition?

Secondly, the Syrians seem, in the light of the recent controversy over the scheme of unity with Iraq, to have serious objections to the monarchical form of government. They have experienced the republican form of government established by France and they

171

seem to have acquired a preference for this system after they had won their independence. With regard to Jordan's undemocratic system of government, where the Constitution has given such power to the King as to render Parliament merely an obsequious assembly, the Syrians regard themselves as having developed a democratic system of government incompatible with Jordan's traditions.

Thirdly, King Abdullah, who untiringly has reiterated that he was working to achieve a national ideal, has been reproached for his advocacy of Syrian unity as merely seeking his own personal glory in order to sit on the throne of Damascus. King Abdullah replied, with a proper show of public spirit, that he was not seeking personal interest but trying to serve Arab national interests. As to the form of government, the King plausibly argued that that will be left to the Syrian people to decide.

In the light of the recent Syrian experiences with military coups, the Syrian people are obviously not left free to decide their fate. Objections to the monarchical regime, strong as they were, seem to be exaggerated by Syria's objections to King Abdullah himself and to the Hashimi family which has suffered loss of prestige since the death of Faysal I.

With regard to the Syro-Iraqi unity scheme, some of the objections raised against the Greater Syria plan would obviously apply to that scheme too, such as the monarchical form of government and Iraq's treaty with Great Britain. Iraq, however, offered to accept such form of union with Syria which would maintain her republican form of government, and which would also keep Syria immune from Iraq's treaty obligations to Great Britain. There is, it is true, a certain apprehension that once the movement of unity is set in motion, the monarchical parties will gain strength at the expense of the republican groupings and Syria may eventually be dragged by Iraq towards a new orientation in her foreign policy.

The rivalry between the Saudi-Egyptian and the Hashimi blocs must be given its due proportion in preventing the achievement of both the Greater Syria and the Syrio-Iraqi unity schemes. While opposition to Greater Syria by the Saudi-Egyptian bloc was justified on the grounds that Jordan, by trying to force her scheme against the wishes of the Syrians, was violating Article 8 of the

Arab Pact (which prevents a member state of the Arab League from interference in the form of government of other member states), the Saudi-Egyptian bloc has afforded itself freedom of intervention in the Syro-Iraqi scheme which it denied to the Hashimi bloc. The Zionist threat, which is probably facing the Fertile Crescent more directly than Egypt and Saudi Arabia, was the chief motive which prompted Syria to contemplate joining Iraq. The intervention of the Saudi-Egyptian bloc by offering Syria support against such a threat has undoubtedly postponed, if not indefinitely prevented, the unity of the Fertile Crescent countries. In case of a more serious threat from the north, such as that of the Soviet Union, a strong and united Fertile Crescent, if it enjoyed the support of the Arab League (by its Collective Security Pact) rather than opposition by the Saudi-Egyptian bloc, could offer more effective resistance to such a threat and would certainly be a stronger barrier to communism and fifth-columnist activities. General Nuri as-Sa'id, in his speech on the Syro-Iraqi unity scheme given in Baghdad (7 March 1950), went so far as to argue that his chief motive for advocating unity with Syria was his fear of communism, whether it came from the north (Russia) or west (Israel).[76]

Apart from the solidarity and strength that might be created against foreign threat, a general Fertile Crescent unity might also help to shift the focus of attention from inter-Arab rivalries into the more constructive and urgently needed social-economic reforms (which have received little attention) by exploiting the inner resources of the area and attracting foreign investment. A political superstructure embracing the various Fertile Crescent entities will not only eliminate the economic barriers among them but might also help to accumulate larger native capital for economic development. Further, internal stability throughout the area, as well as security for foreign capital, seems to be necessary before any foreign help, such as President Truman's Point Four Program and the United Nations technical assistance, could be effectively used. While guarantee against the recurrence of warfare in the Arab World has been given by the Big Three (25 March 1950),[77] a more positive effort to induce the Arabs to coördinate their activities to inaugurate social-economic reforms seems to be urgent. A politico-economic integration of the Fertile Crescent countries might be regarded as a move for the Arabs of this area to keep their house in order.

NOTES

1. Musa al-Alami, *Ibrat Filastin* (Beirut, 1949), p. 52. A condensed translation of this book is to be found in *The Middle East Journal,* 3 (October 1949), 373–405.

2. *The Times,* 30 May 1941.

3. Amir Abdullah's scheme of Syrian unity will be fully discussed in the following section.

4. General Nuri as-Sa'id, *Arab Independence and Unity* (Baghdad, Government Press, 1943), pp. 11–12.

5. *Ibid.,* p. 12.

6. For a discussion of the background and structure of the Arab League, see my "Towards an Arab Union: The League of Arab States," *American Political Science Review,* 40 (February 1946), 90–100; and "The Arab League as a Regional Arrangement," *American Journal of International Law,* 40 (October 1946), 756–777.

7. As early as 1916 Colonel T. E. Lawrence said about Abdullah: "He is obviously working to establish the greatness of the family, and has large ideas, which no doubt include his own particular advancement," *The Arab Bulletin,* 26 November 1916 (reprinted in Lawrence's *Secret Dispatches from Arabia* [London, 1939], p. 37).

8. [Government of Transjordan], the *Jordan White Book on Greater Syria* (Amman, National Press, 1947), pp. 19–20, 22–23 (in Arabic).

9. See the High Commissioner's reply to Amir Abdullah, *ibid.,* pp. 20–21.

10. *Ibid.,* pp. 33–35.

11. *Ibid.,* p. 36.

12. *Ibid.,* p. 38.

13. *Ibid.,* pp. 39–40.

14. *Ibid.,* p. 41.

15. *Ibid.,* pp. 48–49.

16. *Ibid.,* pp. 49–52.

17. See Amir Abdullah's instruction to his Prime Minister in Abdullah's *Memoirs* (Jerusalem, 1945), pp. 200–203, and *Transjordan's White Book on Greater Syria,* pp. 101–103.

18. See also *Abdullah's Memoirs,* pp. 237–249; and *White Book,* pp. 75–77.

19. See an interview of Habib Jamati with the Patriarch in *Akhbar al-Yawm* (Cairo, 3 November 1945).

20. See *al-Makshuf* (Beirut, 31 August 1944), p. 21.

21. *Jordan's White Book* on Greater Syria, pp. 240 and 247.

22. *Jordan's White Book,* p. 250; *Documents on Greater Syria* (Cairo, 1946), p. 25 (in Arabic).

23. *Jordan's White Book*, pp. 252–254; *Documents on Greater Syria*, pp. 27–29.

24. *Documents on Greater Syria*, p. 32; the above statement is reproduced in *Jordan's White Book*, p. 285.

25. *Jordan's White Book*, pp. 256–257; only a brief statement is reproduced in *Documents on Greater Syria*, p. 32.

26. A large selection of articles written in Syria during 1946–47 against the Greater Syria plan were published by the *Dunyah* Magazine in a book entitled, *This Is Greater Syria* (Damascus, 1947). (In Arabic.)

27. See the verbatim minutes of the Syrian Parliament in *Documents on Greater Syria*, pp. 33–52.

28. *Jordan's White Book*, pp. 259–260.

29. *Documents on Greater Syria*, p. 61.

30. *Jordan's White Book*, p. 267; *Documents on Greater Syria*, p. 64.

31. *Jordan's White Book*, p. 266.

32. *Documents on Greater Syria*, pp. 65–66.

33. *Jordan's White Book*, pp. 270–276.

34. Speech of His Excellency Shukri al-Quwatli, President of the Syrian Republic on 15 September 1947 (Beirut, al-Ahad Press, 1947), pp. 8–12.

35. *Al-Ahram*, Cairo, 11 February 1946; and the *Times*, London, 20 September 1946.

36. See text of the Treaty in *The Middle East Journal*, 1 (October 1947), 449–451.

37. The main points of criticism were (1) for permitting the military intervention of one party in the internal affairs of the other; and (2) fear of foreign influence in Iraqi affairs through Transjordan. See Kamil al-Chadirchi, "What Is Behind the Treaty Between Iraq and Transjordan?" (*Sawt Al-Ahali, Baghdad*, 23 April 1947).

38. Probably the Middle East bloc would have been more of a reality if Turkey had approached Egypt, as the leading Arab League country, rather than Iraq.

39. See *Report of the Anglo-American Committee of Inquiry regarding the Problems of European Jewry and Palestine* (London, His Majesty's Stationery Office, 1946), Cmd. 6808.

40. For a summary of the two notes, see *Arab News Bulletin*, London, 26 July and 9 August, 1946.

41. The two reservations made by Iraq and Transjordan were not the same though the objective was probably identical. Iraq objected to the League's resolution on the ground that it did not make reference of the Palestine question to the UN conditional on a previous understanding with Great Britain and the United States on the future status of Palestine. Transjordan's reservation was to the effect that while she agreed to coöperate fully with the other Arab states in defending Palestine, she would like to reserve herself the "freedom of independent action" owing to her special relations and the geographical propinquity to Palestine. See the verbatim minutes of the meeting of the Council of the Arab League on 23 March 1947 in *al-Isbu'*, 4 April 1947.

42. General Nuri's statement was severely criticized in the following day by the press. See *Sawt al-Ahali*, 25 March 1947.

175

43. Musa al-Alami, *op. cit.*, p. 48.

44. See Alford Carleton, "The Syrian Coups d'Etat of 1949," *The Middle East Journal*, 4 (January 1950), 1–11.

45. See text of Proclamation No. 5 issued by Colonel Sami al-Hinnawi on 14 August 1949, (*al-Hayat*, Beirut, 17 August 1949). See also Alford Carleton, "The Syrian Coups d'État," *Middle East Journal*, 4 (January 1950), p. 8.

46. *Al-Ahram*, Cairo, 2 January 1950.

47. See text of a memorandum to this effect submitted by the People's Party to President Quwatli on 10 December 1948 (*al-Hayat*, Beirut, 17 August 1949).

48. Hasan al-Hakim paid a flying visit to Amman shortly after the second coup. A return visit was made to Damascus by Transjordan's Minister of Education, al-Shunqayti. See *al-Ba'th*, Damascus, 21 and 23 November 1949.

49. *al-Ahram*, Cairo, 30 December 1949.

50. *al-Ahram*, 4 February 1950.

51. It was alleged that Sami al-Hinnawi, Commander-in-Chief of the Syrian Army, tried indirectly to influence the elections but without much success. (See Proceedings of the Constituent Assembly in *The Official Gazette*, Vol. 32, 13 April 1950, 238.) Hinnawi, on the other hand, declared at the time of the elections that the army had nothing to do with the elections save for "maintaining security and combatting mischief-doing" (see a statement to this effect by Sami al-Hinnawi in *al-Kifah al-Jadid*, Damascus, 12 November 1949).

52. *The New York Times*, 17 November 1949.

53. For text of the new electoral law see Government of Syria, *Official Gazette*, vol. 31 (12 September 1949), part 1, pp. 2617–2621.

54. For Proceedings of the Constituent Assembly, see *The Official Gazette*, vol. 32 (5 January 1950), part 3, pp. 1–10.

55. *Ibid.*, pp. 46–49.

56. *Ibid.*, pp. 52–53, 55.

57. *Ibid.*, pp. 53–55, 56–57, 59–60.

58. *Ibid.*, p. 65.

59. *Ibid.*, p. 68.

60. *Ibid.*, p. 72.

61. *Ibid.*, pp. 229 ff.

62. *al-Ahram*, 27 December 1949.

63. Proceedings of the Constituent Assembly, *The Official Gazette*, vol. 31 (16 February 1950), part 3, pp. 89–90.

64. *Ibid.*, pp. 105, 108.

65. *al-Ahram.* 9 December 1949, and 10 January 1950.

66. Syrian Government, *The Loan and Commercial Agreements Signed by the Syrian Republic and the Saudi-Arabian Kingdom on 29 January 1950* (Damascus, 1950). (In Arabic.)

67. Proceedings, *Official Gazette*, vol. 32 (13 March 1950), part 3, p. 174.

68. *Ibid.*, p. 170.

69. See a trenchant but vulgar attack by Khalil Kannah in *al-Ahd*, Baghdad, 4 February 1950.

70. *Al-Zaman*, Baghdad, 10 February 1950.

71. See a speech by Lufti al-Haffar, a former Syrian Prime Minister, on the occasion of King Ghazi's death in 1939 (*al-Istiqlal*, Baghdad, 16 May 1939).

72. See Amir Chekib Arslan, *Arab Unity* (Damascus, 1937); and Yusuf Haykal, *Towards Arab Unity* (Cairo, 1943). (Both in Arabic.) See also Edmond Rabbath, *Unité Syrienne et devenir Arabe* (Paris, 1937), pp. 33 ff.

73. *This Is Greater Syria* (Compilation of Press Articles, Damascus, 1947), pp. 115–117, 118–122, 131–134. See also *al-Musawwar*, Cairo, 19 July 1946, and 16 August 1946.

74. For the origins and settlement of the Alexandretta problem, see M. Khadduri, "The Alexandretta Dispute," *American Journal of International Law*, 39 (July 1945), 406–425.

75. *Jordan's White Book* on Greater Syria, pp. 47, 85, 96–97.

76. General Nuri, in dividing the world into democratic and communistic camps, stated that the position of Israel is still uncertain, but he thought that Israel is very likely to choose the communist side, hence the Arab World would be threatened by communism from the north and west. See text of General Nuri's speech in *al-Sha'b*, Baghdad, 8 March 1950.

77. For text of the joint declaration of England, France, and the United States, see *The New York Times*, 26 March 1950. The Arab League states, while accepting the substance of the declaration, made the reservation that it should not be construed to mean that the Big Three have regarded the area under their protection or that the Near East has been divided into zones of influence. For the text of the Arab League reply, see *al-Ahram*, 22 June, 1950.

MOSHE PERLMANN

Notes on Labor in Egypt, 1950

Labor is a factor of growing importance in Egypt. The following is an attempt to sketch its role and problems during 1950 on the basis of reports in the Egyptian press.

Labor unrest and unionism made their bow on the Nile a half century ago, but it is only thirty years ago that the beginnings of political laborist agitation can be easily discerned. In the 1930's local industry expanded under a protective tariff wall, and the growing body of industrial labor was drawn into political party struggles when a prince of the royal house assumed the role of labor organizer—only to face the rivalry of various groups, in particular the Wafd party jealous of any mass force outside its own ranks. The recent war brought about considerable industrial expansion; masses of workers were employed by the Allies; the U.S.S.R. established an embassy in Cairo; and the East-West ideological conflict far from cooling in the shade of the pyramids engulfed circles of the local intelligentsia. The last five years have been marked by a high tide of activity in the ranks of labor and the intelligentsia, on both the unionist and political planes.

Labor legislation, especially since 1940, forbids organization on a national scale and prohibits unions among rural laborers—the bulk of the wage earners—and among certain categories of urban labor. The unions have shown an unstable registered membership of about 120,000, and another 50,000 to 60,000 are within their sphere of influence.[1] In view of the fact that in 1946 the average weekly wage in industry was L.E. 1¼ ($5 at the time) for 51 hours of work, and the cost of living was about triple the prewar level, there seemed to be ample opportunities for union activity.[2]

But the series of labor conflicts that began with the end of the war were on the political level, and the influence of intellectuals in them is unmistakable. Leftist publications appeared in rapid succession. Action committees, first of workers, then of students, were set up and joined in an attempt to establish a labor federation on a national scale. This agitation was used by the authorities as a pretext for measures of suppression in 1947. Mass arrests, suspension of publications, searches, and trials drove the non-union segments of the agitation underground. The war in Palestine and the suppression of the wide-flung movement of the Moslem Brotherhood tightened the system of suppression, and cases of "destructive elements" were transferred to military tribunals which gave sentences of hard labor from two to five years to arrested agitators, while administrative suspicion sent hundreds to concentration camps without trial.

Elements of radicalism as well as socialism in Egypt go back to the scholarly essayist Ya'qub Sarruf (1852–1927) [3] and the Copt writer Salama Musa who was influenced by G. B. Shaw. In the period between the two wars a small but ever-widening group of Egyptian students at home and abroad studied the social sciences, and was attracted by the European socialist movements—and by the salvation made in Moscow. British laborism was too much part and parcel of the axiomatically hated imperialist system; indeed it was especially with labor governments that Egyptian negotiators failed in their struggle for the evacuation of British troops and completion of independence. European labor at the same time was woefully neglectful of colonial and dependent territories. On the other hand, the brashness, freshness, and unhindered logic of Soviet anti-imperialism of those days seemed very acceptable to Egyptian intellectuals. In the forties, a number of studies on Egypt's social problems by leftists and non-leftists became the source of a wave of social critique which steadily gathered momentum. The woes of the *fellahin*—this teeming mass of the bulk of the Egyptian people—overpopulation, redistribution of land, and industrialization, were added to the typical roster of older problems: British evacuation, the Sudan, political reforms, and modernization. If the old roster was a springboard for lashing out at

179

the British, and even foreigners in general, the new issues proved a source of internal criticism against the powers that be—Egypt's upper classes, now denounced as henchmen of foreign imperialism.

During the war a poll of Cairo students showed that some 60 per cent voted for collectivism; 18 per cent of these were for Islamic socialism and the rest divided between socialism and communism. The pressure of the moods and activities of this youth, of the labor movement, and of their opposite number—the Moslem Brotherhood—no doubt hastened the ripening of social consciousness and social responsibility, noticeable of late in the upper strata.[4]

The high cost of living and restlessness among workers induced the government to issue a decree under military law adding special cost-of-living allowances to wages.[5] Some factories accepted the measure and introduced this allowance for their workers, while others doubted whether it applied to them, or argued that they were unable to carry out the decree. The Minister of the Interior, Fu'ad Siraj al-Din, declared the decree sheer necessity, and reminded the senate of the mood of the workers before and since the decree was issued, mentioning that company profits had increased by 8 million pounds the preceding year. The Minister of Social Affairs, Dr. Ahmad Husayn, revealed the discrepancy between the slow rise in wages and the more rapid rise in prices. "Company directors raised their own salaries (since 1939) 500 per cent; why not add 150 per cent to workers' take-home pay? It is a matter of justice. Furthermore, production will increase with the improvement in the position of the worker." (Quoted from *al-Ahram* April 13, 1950.) The Ministry of Social Affairs assured workers that they would obtain the allowance; consequently 80 per cent of the manufacturers and merchants carried out the decree. The Minister received a labor delegation and advised them against listening to elements agitating among them for disorder. Workers organized a series of strikes and sit-in strikes demanding payment of the cost-of-living allowance, and sometimes violence or threats of violence figured in the news reports. The Labor Department of the Ministry rallied officials to the support of workers, urging more food, safety measures, medical service, clubs, efforts toward higher production, and insurance. It also attempted to direct trade union education, and urged the use of wall newspapers in the factories.

On the international scene, since 1936 Egypt has been a member of the ILO, and since 1945 she has held a seat on the executive committee. She now hopes to have an assistant directorship and a special Middle East office to be maintained in Cairo. Egypt has joined 6 out of 98 agreements on labor worked out under the ILO.* In 1949 Egypt contributed about $65,000 to the ILO.

To return to the home front; in the Chamber of Deputies party-bickering has recently brought about attacks on the government in connection with labor affairs and the position of the vast under-privileged masses. The budget, according to one deputy, does not reflect the needs of the poor for medical assistance. Furthermore, there is no move on the part of the government to limit working hours and to introduce a minimum wage. Several bills were introduced to set a low maximum in land property, while the freezing of rural rents was suggested.

Radical trends among intellectuals, white-collar workers, and educated youth are widespread in Egypt today, and measures of suppression are hardly likely to succeed. The correspondent of the London *Times* (June 16, 1950) recently described the attitudes prevailing in Egypt thus: "Repression, spasmodic charity, reluctant and limited application of comprehensive paper social programmes, and an easy attitude of 'it can't happen here,' often expressed in the wishful belief that Muslims are immune from Communist blandishments . . ."

The London *Times* writer further remarked:

Egypt would appear to be the best breeding ground for Communists in the Middle East. The gap between rich and poor is enormous, social conscience is still rudimentary . . . There is a growing artisan class, the beginnings of a trade union movement, an overcrowded and rapidly increasing land-hungry peasantry. There is also a large output of students, most of whom are idealistic and emotionally frustrated by lack of opportunity, and genuinely anxious to improve the state of their countrymen. They are excellent instruments for nation-wide propa-

* Francis O. Wilcox, of the Senate Foreign Relations Committee, remarked that the United States has ratified about the same number of International Labor Organization conventions as Egypt.

ganda, since they come from every village, and their education commands the attention of the simple illiterate countryfolk.

It must not be forgotten that communism is illegal and its followers must work subversively in the underground.[6]

Subversion includes infiltration into various legal bodies. According to a communist statement, the petty bourgeois who are still in the Wafd will not find it any longer the fighting party it used to be. Disappointed, all these lawyers, students, and writers could be influenced. Communists, it is stated, should activate them, but should be careful not to exaggerate their importance lest they, the communists, fall prey to a rightist deviation. At present they should expose the Wafd's preparation for a treaty with Britain and thus strengthen the internal rift in the ranks of the Wafd. They should further act in organizations such as those of lawyers, students, engineers, and so forth.

Who are the communists? In Alexandria, it was found that 50 per cent of them were students, 10 per cent were professionals, and 40 per cent, workers. There are among them communist members of minority groups: Armenians, Greeks, Jews. Sometimes an issue is made of that too: it is the wicked aliens who pervert the youth.

What do the communist activities consist of? Cells previously of three to five and now of two to three persons discuss publications; they reproduce or publish leaflets and pamphlets—printed, typewritten, mimeographed, or handwritten—on various matters of public interest, and distribute these in schools, factories, and on streets. In Gaza and Rafah, they wrote against "pharaonic imperialism." They wrote that the rich are the enemy of the people; Red China is saluted; Russia and Stalin are enthusiastically praised. Such are the contents of an issue of the sixteen-page monthly *Voice of the Proletariat*. Various organizations, including trade unions, are infiltrated and a few trusted men become members of the communist cells. Apparently there are three important groups groping towards the establishment of a unified party on a national scale: the Egyptian Communist Organization, the group called "Toward an Egyptian Communist Party," and the "Democratic Movement for National Liberation." They use their initials, and a number of other abbreviations, and a code in which "specialist" designates a member, "patient," a worker, "the hospital Qasr al Ayni," the Cairo branch, "microbe," a policeman. (*Akhbar al-Yaum* April 8, 1950.)

Their committees try to maintain several apartments, meet at night, and telephone the anti-communist squad's officers just before a meeting is to take place to ascertain if the officers are on their jobs. In some city quarter a new dweller will appear, a pleasant person. He will draft a letter about defects of sanitation in the neighborhood and call on people for signatures, talk to women who in turn will discuss the matter with their men, and thus agitation is started. Members are especially careful on the eve of May Day when police vigilance is to be expected.

In prison, in concentration camps and courts, communists follow the prescribed line. They refuse to answer questions in military courts because they demand that the Wafd government carry out its promise to abolish the vestiges of the state of siege, and that their cases be transferred to civil courts. If they give explanations, they parade as ardent patriots fighting for the evacuation of the British and unification of the Nile Valley, and the President of the Court is bound to admit that he and his colleagues are in full agreement with the defendants.

The government is not prepared to give up its special right to deal with those suspected of communist activity; and special legislation is to be passed against such political suspects. The Association of Lawyers, however, opposes this as an unconstitutional infraction of the freedom of thought. A lonely Wafdist even voiced the opinion that it might be simpler to fight a legalized Communist Party, but the cabinet insists on the new law.

Under this law of suspicion, hard labor for not more than ten years threatens those found guilty of establishing, organizing, or administering societies working toward class rule and changes in the social regime. Imprisonment may be coupled with fines from L.E. 100 to L.E. 1,000, especially if terrorism was preached. The authorities plan a special office in the Ministry of the Interior that would direct the ideological struggle against "destructive principles" especially among the younger generation, with the conviction that an idea can be fought only by ideas.

At the same time everyone is parading of late as a socialist. Right and left, old and young, modernist and anti-modernist, Wafd and anti-Wafd, all claim to be socialists. F. Siraj al-Din, lieutenant of the Prime Minister, stated that the Wafd was a Socialist Party. Even the small National Party is not opposed to nationalization. A university professor explained that Egypt is possibly more advanced in socialism than laborite Britain, for railways, telegraphs, schools, are government-owned, and this ownership is slowly but surely expanding, while in Britain the advance is too rapid and does not allow for mental adjustment, giving the workers the impression that they must always expect further increases in their wages and reductions in their working hours. Almost as a dissonance comes the statement of the well-known physician, diplomat, and industrialist, Dr. Affifi, that strangely enough everybody seems to be going in for socialism in Egypt precisely at a time when Britain doubts it, France is getting rid of it, and Italy repudiates it. He maintains that Egypt's trouble is low productivity, not private ownership, and in regard to state socialism, Egypt has had enough of it under the Ptolemies and the Romans, the Mamelukes and the Turks (referring evidently to systems of state monopolies).

The world press informs its readers that recent elections brought into the Egyptian Parliament the first and only Socialist Party deputy. He really represents an old group under a new name. The new name is the Socialist Party, or even the Socialist Democratic Party, but this is the old group—Young Egypt (Green Shirts) under Ahmad Husayn, with its extreme nationalism, Islamic tendency, and Fascist outlook.[7] The party, however, will demand nationalization of industry, redistribution of wealth, and the introduction of minimum standards. Its further demands repeat the general national slogans, from the evacuation of the British to electrification. A newspaper, *Misr al Fatat,* serves as its organ.

Another group, the Labor Party, under the patronage of Prince Abbas Halim, also decided to call itself the Socialist Labor Party and hoped to rally not only the workers but all reform and socialist-minded people.

The main problem is whether and how labor and leftists will find their path to the vast impoverished mass of the peasantry whose bulk consists of wage-earners, hired laborers without any land or with pigmy plots,[8] the masses whose rise to political life must transform some day social relations and the body politic in the Nile Valley.[9]

BIBLIOGRAPHY

Charles Issawi, *Egypt* (London, 1947).

A. A. J. el-Gritly, "The Structure of Modern Industry in Egypt," (Cairo, 1948), in *L'Égypte Contemporaine*, Nos. 241–242.

"The Industrial Census in 1945," in *Economic Bulletin*, National Bank of Egypt (Cairo, October 1948).

H. Butler, *Report on Labour Conditions in Egypt* (Cairo, 1932).

Egyptian Government, Ministry of Finances, Statistical Dept., *Statistics of Wages and Working Hours in Egypt*, July 1946 (Cairo, 1947); also Jan. 1948 (Cairo, 1949).

Aharon Cohen, *The Arab Labour Movement* (Tel Aviv, 1947). (In Hebrew.)

Committee on Foreign Affairs, *National and International Communism in the Near East* (Washington, 1948).

M. Colombe, "Deux Années d'Histoire de l'Égypte," in *Politique Etrangère* (May 1947).

Z. Badaoui, *Les Problèmes du Travail et les Organisations Ouvrières en Égypte* (Alexandria, 1948).

W. J. Handley, "The Labor Movement in Egypt," in *The Middle East Journal* (July 1949).

M. Perlmann, "Labor in Egypt," in *Palestine Affairs* (New York, July 1949).

R. Barawi and M. H. Alish, *Economic Evolution of Egypt in Modern Times* (4 ed.; Cairo, 1949), ch. 9. (In Arabic.)

R. Butrus, *Exposition of the Law of Individual Labor Contract* (Cairo, 1950). (In Arabic.)

NOTES

1. An Egyptian official stated that there are about 125,000 organized workers in 478 unions. In Geneva, Egyptian delegates stated to the ILO that in 1948 there was an estimated registration of 124,000. (*Al-Ahram*, September 7, 1949, and June 20, 1949.)

2. The book *Statistics of Wages and Working Hours in Egypt*, January 1948 (Cairo, 1949), shows an average weekly wage of L.E. 1.39 for 51 hours of work; 45.9 per cent of the workers earned less than L.E. 1, and 34.5 per cent less than L.E. 2; i.e., 80 per cent earned less than L.E. 2 per week. The cost of living rose during January-June 1950 from 281.5

(1939 = 100) to 289.5 (*National Bank of Egypt, Economic Bulletin*, 3, No. 3, p. 212). What with the results of the sterling devaluation, price increases mean that the value of the Egyptian pound now is about 30 per cent of what it was in 1939. (*N. Y. Times*, Jan. 9, 1951).

3. C. Brockelmann, *Geschichte der arabischen Litteratur* (Leiden, 1942), S III, 215 ff.

4. *Times*, London, July 16, 1950.

5. R. Butrus, *Exposition of the Law of Individual Labor Contract*, pp. 226–231.

6. The following of the Communists is therefore difficult to gauge. A United States Congressional document estimated it at "some 5,000 active members organized in several hundred cells imbedded in government bureaus, the universities, police, army, even the reactionary Moslem Brethren and the great theological university of the Azhar."

7. Charles P. Issawi, *Egypt*, p. 175; James Heyworth-Dunne, *Religious and Political Trends in Modern Egypt* (Washington, D.C., 1950), pp. 103–105; M. Colombe, *Cahiers*, etc., pp. 23–24; also *Oriente Moderno* (Rome, 1940), pp. 183–188. The leader, Ahmad Husayn, published two pamphlets in New York. His organ was suspended in January 1951.

8. D. Warriner, *Land and Poverty in the Middle East* (London, 1948), pp. 38–39.

9. The Korean affair, what with the neutral stand taken by the Egyptian government, gave rise to violent discussions. The arguments for intervention in Korea sound like those that led to the British occupation of Egypt and the Sudan; just as the followers of Arabi in the 1880's were the people of Egypt, so the communists are the people of Korea: such is the judgment of the weekly, *Ruz al Yusuf* (July 18 1950). The former ambassador in Moscow, Muh. Kamil al-Bondari Pasha, is no less definite in his strong pro-Soviet position (*al-Ahram*, July 7, 1950). It is evidently against him that M. Tabi'i writes when he accuses a distinguished Egyptian personage of being instrumental in the encouragement of insolent oral and printed propaganda by communists. The latter now prefer to spend money on intellectuals, educated youth, officials (even in the police and in the army). "Thus, young officers," continues Tabi'i, "especially after the revelations of corruption (armament deals), will fall prey to leftist talk. I am fully sensible of the seriousness of this statement; 90 per cent of these people do not show any positive inclination for communism, but out of rejection of present conditions will be driven into the arms of the leftists. All cabinets, the whole regime, work for the benefit of the left. Nepotism, partisanship, corruption, bribery, speculations, ostentatious squandering of wealth are thrown into relief by the people's state of health, education, welfare." (*Akhir Sa'a*, August 9, 1950).

The "peace campaign" spread to Egypt, and a number of distinguished personages supported it. It seems that the various communist groups merged finally into the Egyptian Communist Party established towards the end of 1950 (*Akhbar al-Yaum*, Jan. 27, 1951). In the last weeks of 1950 the rising cost of living caused a new wave of strikes.

Remarks by Charles P. Issawi

Almost the only source of information about communism in the Near East, and especially in Egypt, used by Mr. Perlmann has been the newspapers. From the Egyptian newspapers one would gather that communists are all over the country in great numbers, but from American newspapers one might conclude that the United States was honeycombed with communist cells.

One must remember that the communist movement in Egypt started as a movement of intellectuals. Trade unions were given official recognition by the government only in 1942, and this recognition has helped to distinguish the union people from intellectuals. It has also kept the unions from communist domination. Since the Wafdist party came to power early in 1950, the number of strikes has decreased. This indicates that the labor movement is not irrevocably dedicated to revolutionary action and methods. Rather the labor unions have been trying to improve the conditions of its members, and of labor in general. Labor in Egypt is prepared to trust the government if it feels that the government is sympathetic to it.

Everyone in Egypt calls himself a socialist, but this is a sign of the times. It shows a country approaching a certain stage of development, perhaps comparable to the American "New Deal." Dr. Bonné, eminent Israeli economist, said that people in underdeveloped countries think more in socialist terms than in terms of western liberal capitalism. In Turkey, the Arab states, Iran, and even India, the government is bound to play a greater role in the economic development of these countries. There is a long tradition of government activity in all of these states. So in Egypt when people call themselves socialists it does mean something and is not a mere word.

The spread of communism is a normal concomitant of industrialization. In the Near East it has developed only in large towns, in the oil fields, or in areas in which Soviet policy has promoted nationalism together with communism, such as Azerbaijan and parts of Kurdistan. So communism is quite localized in the Near East. Generally speaking, the incidence of communism is proportionate to the degree of urbanization. Thus, according to a recent publication of the House of Representatives, the communists of Israel are the best organized in the Near East.

It is not so much internal factors which will decide the fate of communism in the Near East as the respective attitudes of the United States and the Soviet Union. Of course internal factors are important too and a combination of them with external developments will determine the fate of communism in this area.

One point which should be stressed is the importance of rural labor, and the efforts being made to improve its lot. The Egyptian government is trying to do something in the countryside where the mass of the people live. First, the government has reduced the burden of the land tax on small farmers. Then it has distributed some state domains among the peasants. This has been a gradual process but accelerated since the end of World War II. Over one million acres of wasteland are to be improved by companies and then distributed to farmers in small plots. Another encouraging sign is the coöperative movement which has increased tenfold in the last ten years in Egypt. The government has consistently fostered this, and recently the Agricultural Credit Bank was transformed by the government into a Coöperative Bank. Almost one-third of the peasants today belong to coöperatives. Over a hundred village centers have been created since the first one was founded in 1941. Each center serves a population of about ten thousand. So almost a million peasants have the benefits of the village center. In each one there is a doctor, a social worker, an agronomist, and other experts. As a result of their work, incomes have been raised because of the improved methods of farming and protection of health. The coöperation of the peasants, of course, is necessary for the success of the village center, and the response has been very encouraging, for the peasants have contributed labor and money for the common good.

REMARKS BY CHARLES P. ISSAWI

At present there is a draft law on social insurance before the Egyptian parliament. It is unique for this region and compares favorably with the advanced social legislation of western states. Unemployed, and families which have lost their breadwinner, will receive financial assistance from the government; and other forms of social insurance are provided. In short, the government is doing a great deal to improve conditions of labor in Egypt.

The United Nations have also worked in the Near East. The Food and Agriculture Organization has held conferences and established schools. Services in health have also been rendered. For the first time in history, something is being done in the Near Eastern countryside.

CONCLUSION

H. A. R. GIBB

Conclusion

The experience of every conference that really comes to the point, in which, that is to say, there is a real meeting of minds, is that those taking part in it tend gradually to concentrate their thinking on a particular aspect of the topic that they have assembled to discuss. That, I believe, has been happening during this conference. We have been coming gradually to realize that the ultimate problem which we are facing is how to get the ideas and the objectives of democracy across to the peoples of the Near East, and what that means for us and for them.

We have, in fact, been trying to interpret democracy to the peoples of the Near East throughout the nineteenth century and up to the present time in terms of our own active practice of democracy, and rather in its etymological sense of government by the people. We have been inclined to imagine that it was quite enough to set up democratic institutions of our own brand. This is, I think, what Mr. Harvey Hall meant when he said that the British, by setting up monarchical institutions with Parliaments, had frozen the Near East in a static situation. That statement I thought at the time curious and even perverse, but on thinking it over I have come to believe that there is an element of truth in it.

We have introduced our own institutions because we think of democracy in terms of our own institutions, whether they are monarchical or republican, party systems, spoils systems, and all. We have not sufficiently realized that none of our countries are strictly democratic. Democracy is an objective, an aim, which we are trying to reach through our systems. It is a developing idea, and the forms which it may take are not limited to any one sort or kind of organization. For instance, the "Welfare State" is a new form, a new definition, of democracy which some countries in Western Europe, and particularly Great Britain, are trying to introduce.

To put it very briefly, democracy has to be interpreted not so much as government of the people, by the people, but above all, as in Lincoln's phrase, government "for the people." If we are to get democracy across to the Near East as something which will appeal to its peoples, something that will make sense, then we have to interpret democracy as service. But we have to be convinced of this in ourselves and see it realized among ourselves before we can project it to others. The first problem for us is how we are going to interpret in our own community life this conception of democracy as service.

The people of the United States have made a massive and unexampled effort in this direction during the postwar years. They have not yet been entirely successful, though, in their endeavor, because the actions and the motives that are adduced for the actions do not always tally. I do not think it has yet got across in Western Europe, and certainly not in Asia, that what the American government and the American people are trying to do is to serve not their own interests pure and simple, but to serve the interests of the peoples who are benefiting by the immense efforts that they are making. The suspicion that prevents this from getting across is, I think, due to the fact that they are not associated with democracy as a body of ideas which aims to serve the interests of the world, but interpreted as the action of a country with a particular form of democratic government which is interested in securing, first and foremost, its own political objectives.

This is the lesson, and the problem, which come out of our conference, and I have no solution to give here to the problem. To repeat: how are we to find the forms and the phrases by which we can symbolize to the peoples of Asia this conception of democracy as service? How can we remove the suspicions which have been generated, even sometimes in Western Europe, but above all in Asia, that "democracy" is simply a cover for all sorts of private aims and objectives? Until we do find the solution, we must expect the East to remain suspicious of all our arguments and claims on behalf of democracy, and of our encouragements to establish the democratic idea in the world at large. However briefly and unsatisfactorily I have tried to put this forward, I believe that it is the real meaning of what we have been trying to do here.

APPENDICES

Appendix I. Discussions

DISCUSSIONS

The questions which Dr. Bunche asked the various speakers during the second and third nights of the Conference, and their answers, are included in Appendix I.

RALPH BUNCHE TO GEORGE MC GHEE:

When we give financial assistance to countries such as those in the Near East, how are we to insure that this assistance really serves the intended purpose? How can we insure that the recipients use it to best advantage, and that the people in the area receive the intended benefits? There are two alternatives, in my opinion. One would be a tough or tougher policy by the giving nation. It would necessarily involve increasing degrees of interference by the United States, which is the main giver, in the internal affairs of Near Eastern countries. The other alternative, one which I think can be much more fully explored than it has been explored, would be to work through the United Nations, where much more might be done with much less suspicion attaching to such actions than in the case of individual nations.

GEORGE C. MC GHEE:

I should like to take this opportunity to say how deeply I was impressed with the sincerity of Dr. Malik's paper. In my opinion it constitutes a most significant statement coming from an outstanding representative of the peoples of the Near East, a statement to which we in the Department of State will give most careful study.

I should like to comment on the question of our generosity in giving assistance and whether it would not be wise to give generously now to forestall later necessities for doing more drastic things. Perhaps the people of the Near East will think we have not been generous. It is quite true that our country in its postwar policy, as a matter of priority, has had to direct its assistance first to Western Europe. We rationalized that at the time, and we hoped that other peoples accepted that rationalization. There is not only the question of priority, however, but the

199

fact which I brought out in my remarks, that there are basic problems to be solved first which are not financial problems. There are barriers to be overcome, which are not in themselves financial in nature, before large sums of money can be utilized effectively. These barriers exist throughout the underdeveloped areas. The question you raise as to how to assure that the sums provided can be spent effectively is a very difficult one. However we have by now accumulated considerable experience with this problem. I am afraid that it will always be true that our people, through the Congress, will demand that American assistance given abroad be spent effectively for the purposes intended, and that Americans exercise some degree of supervision over it. I believe that this feeling is partly a reaction to the UNRRA effort, which has been widely criticized in this country as not having been properly executed. I believe that there would be strong feeling against this government turning over large sums of money, for material assistance to other countries, to the United Nations for administration. I can only say that one must pursue a very cautious course in dealing with problems of assistance in another country, in assuring that funds are used effectively without at the same time infringing on the sovereign rights of the local government or in any way attempting to exert a political influence. I think that our representatives in countries such as Greece, where our economic assistance is vital to the existence of the country, have exhibited a marked restraint in this matter. By and large, the people of Greece have been surprised that we have not intervened more than we in fact have. I would like to point out one final item which I think is extremely important, and it springs from a conversation which Dr. Malik and I had only last week. Dr. Malik said, knowing of my own particular experience with problems of economic assistance, that in his judgment of the things that we could offer the Near East, economic assistance was of less importance than other things which we had to offer. In his paper he has told us of these other things, and I think that if we have a deficiency, as a people, it is in projecting ourselves to other peoples of the world. We have not yet acquired the ability to project ourselves adequately in the spiritual and intellectual fields which Dr. Malik discussed. We have projected ourselves more in the economic and in the military spheres. We have not yet found a way of adequately projecting the real essence of the American feeling and understanding for the other peoples of the world to those peoples, so that they feel, as Dr. Malik in his own words has said, that we have real "love" for them.

RALPH BUNCHE TO CHARLES MALIK:

[The first question is the same as the one asked of Mr. McGhee.] In regard to tensions and fears in the Near East, what significance do the Arab states attach to the Three Power Declaration on the Near East, and to the United Nations intervention with armed force in Korea for the purpose of repelling aggression?

CHARLES MALIK:

Dr. Bunche first asked if this country should offer the Near East large sums of money, and if this act would help in the present situation to cement the friendship of the Near East to this country. I should answer that it certainly would help, provided the money is wisely spent, and I should hope this country would never consent to give money except when it was certain that it would be spent in the best possible way. I think it would be a great help, provided it is spent wisely, but to depend on it alone would be a great mistake, because people everywhere have taken your money and then forgotten about you. Unless a relationship of far deeper trust, confidence, and partnership is evolved, more material help will not be enough. A very charming lady, who returned not long ago from Europe, told me the Europeans are all ungrateful. I asked her why. She said, "We give them billions of dollars and they continue to criticize us." On further reflection, however, she felt that perhaps it wasn't enough to give billions of dollars. You have got to share other things with peoples. This overemphasis on money, financial assistance, and economic development, wonderful as it is, might cause, I would say, more harm than if it did not exist at all in American relations with the Near East. Taken by itself alone it is not good. There ought to be these other things, about which I have spoken, which are more fundamental.

The second question which Dr. Bunche asked related to the Three Power Declaration on the Near East. That Declaration was very important, and I believe in the right direction. I am happy both about the fact that it has been done and the way in which it has been done. But these things, you know, prove themselves only in the doing. I should say that the Three Power Declaration will have significance only two or three years from now, when we really know what France, England, and America will do about it. Of course it does lend itself to half a dozen different possibilities, as every diplomatic statement does, and it depends on the spirit, the intent, and the whole policy behind it. So the Three Power Declaration, good as it is as a beginning, must be followed by implementation.

Now about the Far Eastern situation, the reaction of the Near East so far is slow, and understandably so. In general there is approval of American and United Nations action, but there are outstanding problems in the Near East about which neither the United States nor the United Nations seems to care, and the peoples of the Near East keep on wondering why. Surely the United States and the United Nations must feel as much concern for the implementation of decisions concerning the Near East as for decisions concerning the Far East.

RALPH BUNCHE TO MOSHE KEREN:

What significance does Israel attribute to the recent Three Power Declaration with regard to arms and boundaries between Israel and the Arab states?

MOSHE KEREN:

In answer to Dr. Bunche's question regarding the tripartite announcement on the Near East, let me say that the Declaration was composed of two parts. The first part was concerned with the right of the Near Eastern nations to arm themselves for legitimate self-defense and for internal security, and the three powers declared that they will treat the requests for arms submitted by these countries in the light of these principles. The second part of the declaration threatens any Near Eastern state with sanctions if it should engage in hostile activities against a neighboring state.

The two parts of the declaration are of different value. To start with the second, we believe that the intention of the Western powers to maintain peace in the Near East is genuine, and we definitely believe they mean what they say. The declaration should therefore give the nations of the Near East a feeling of security from aggression. This is certainly true of Israel, and this feeling of safety must apply to the Arab nations, if they have any fear of Israel.

No nation, however, can trust its security to the promises of other powers. In case of a crisis the intervention of an outside agency takes time, and the result is by no means assured. Even the United Nations, as Dr. Bunche well knows, has not always acted in time. So every nation must be prepared.

We do not think that the decision of the Western powers to arm the nations of the Near East was a wise step. We would have thought it wiser for the statesmen of the Western powers to make rearmament conditional on the conclusion of peace in the area.

RALPH BUNCHE TO HARVEY HALL
AND L. I. STRAKHOVSKY:

I should like to ask Mr. Hall whether, in envisaging the future cultural development of the Arab world, he considers it inevitable that all the Arab peoples will follow a similar cultural pattern or whether there may be some significant cultural diversity developing, as for example, between Egypt and Lebanon? Finally I should like to ask Professor Strakhovsky a question, which I might preface by saying that since my return from the Near East last year I have often been asked, why did not the Soviet Union seem to make any serious effort to obstruct the United Nations peace effort in Palestine? I may say only that, though I spent two years in the Holy Land, I became neither a prophet nor the son of a prophet, and certainly would never attempt to prophesy what the Soviet Union might do, or to explain why it had or had not done something, but I could say that all of us who were out there on behalf of the United Nations were very happy that the Soviet Union did not try to obstruct the United Nations effort.

HARVEY HALL:

There is nothing inevitable about the future of the Arabs, any more than with other peoples. Perhaps the most important question in the Near East today is that of unity or disunity. In the political sphere certainly the trend toward disunity is the stronger. One must remember that there are many factors working for political disunity in the Arab world. Some states are desert states; others have had broader contact with the West; some possess large minorities lacking in others; each possesses particular interests of its own.

In cultural matters this is not so markedly the case. The movement for Arab unity has certainly had most success on this basis. There are factors for unity here: all Arabs share a heritage and Cairo affords a cultural center for the Arab world. My guess is that even if political unity does not become stronger, a greater cultural unity is possible— assuming, of course, that the Arab world does not come wholly or in part under the domination of foreign cultures.

L. I. STRAKHOVSKY:

Dr. Bunche said he was neither a prophet nor the son of a prophet. To answer his question I must become a seer with a crystal ball. The motivation of the Soviet Union is often very difficult to perceive, and although the role of the Soviet Union in the settlement in Palestine may seem disinterested, the Soviet Union always has its interests. Contrary to general belief, the Soviet government is very sensitive to outside public opinion. In the Palestine question the Soviet Union did not want to offend the Jews of the world and particularly those in the United States by taking a stand, because the American Jews have been, by and large, favorably inclined toward the Soviets. On the other hand, I think the Soviet Union is staking its hope for a revolution favorable to the Soviet Union in the Near East rather on the Arabs than on the Jews.

Appendix II. Program of the Conference on "The Great Powers and the Near East," held at Harvard University, August 7–9, 1950

MONDAY, AUGUST 7: *The Internal Aims of the Near Eastern Countries.*

AFTERNOON SESSION — *Chairman,* Richard N. Frye, Assistant Professor, Middle Eastern Studies, Harvard University.

PAPER — "Notes on Labor in Egypt, 1950," by Moshe Perlmann, Professor in Islamics, New School of Social Research, New York, and Dropsie College, Philadelphia.

REMARKS — Charles P. Issawi, Secretariat of the United Nations. Francis O. Wilcox, Chief of Staff, Senate Foreign Relations Committee.

EVENING SESSION — *Chairman,* H. A. R. Gibb, Laudian Professor of Arabic, Oxford University.

PAPER — "Some Aspects of Oil in the Middle East," by E. L. DeGolyer, Geologist, Oil Producer, Director, American Petroleum Institute.

PAPER — "The Scheme of Fertile Crescent Unity: A Study in Inter-Arab Relations," by Majid Khadduri, Professor of Middle East Studies, School of Advanced International Studies and The Johns Hopkins University.

REMARKS — George C. Keiser, Chairman, Board of Governors, The Middle East Institute, Washington, D.C.

REMARKS — Ralph Bunche, Chief, Trustees Division, Secretariat of the United Nations.

TUESDAY, AUGUST 8: *The United States and the Near East.*

AFTERNOON SESSION — *Chairman,* Ephraim A. Speiser, Professor of Semitics, University of Pennsylvania.

PAPER   "A Cultural Relations Policy in the Near East," by Mortimer Graves, Executive Secretary, American Council of Learned Societies.

REMARKS   Harvey P. Hall, Editor, *The Middle East Journal.* Richard N. Frye.

EVENING SESSION   *Chairman,* Ephraim A. Speiser.

PAPER   "Israel and the United States," by Moshe Keren, Counselor, Embassy of Israel.

PAPER   "The Pattern of Great Power Impact on the Near East," by Harvey P. Hall.

PAPER   "The Nature of Soviet Propaganda in the Near East," by Leonid I. Strakhovsky, Professor of Russian, University of Toronto.

REMARKS   Ralph Bunche.

WEDNESDAY, AUGUST 9: *The Near East in the World.*

AFTERNOON SESSION   *Chairman,* Edwin M. Wright, United Nations Adviser to the Assistant Secretary of State for Near Eastern, South Asian, and African Affairs.

PAPER   "The United Nations and Palestine," by J. C. Hurewitz, Lecturer at the Center of Israeli Studies, Columbia University, and at the Institute for Israel and the Middle East, Dropsie College.

PAPER   "The Near East in the World," by William Thomson, Professor of Arabic, Harvard University.

REMARKS   Majid Khadduri.

EVENING SESSION   *Chairman,* Edwin M. Wright.

PAPER   "The Near East between East and West," by Charles Malik, Minister of Lebanon to the United States.

PAPER   "Economic Development and the Near East," by George C. McGhee, Assistant Secretary of State for Near Eastern, South Asian, and African Affairs.

PAPER   "The Near Eastern Economy in the World and Its Possibilities of Development," by Charles P. Issawi.

REMARKS   Ralph Bunche.

209

Middle East Institute, 81
Middle East Journal, 82
Mohammed Ali, 63
Mongols, 29
Moscow, peace conference in, 68
Moslems, 19; in the eighteenth century, 35–36
Moslem Brotherhood, suppression of, 179–180
Moslem Caliphate, 28
Mosul, oil reserves of, 127, 131
Mufti of Jerusalem, 168, 169
Musa, Salama, 179
Mutuality, 87

Naples, 25
Napoleonic wars, 25, 35
Near East, definition of, 11–12, 57; stand on communism, 15–16; arming and self-defense, 21; resources, 57–58
Negeb, the, 98, 114
Nehru, Prime Minister, 81
New Time, 68
New York Bond Market, 51
New York Peace Conference, 68
Nicholas, Bishop, 68
North Africa, 28
North Atlantic Pact, 69
Nuri, General as-Sa'id, 139, 156, 167; Arab unity plans of, 139–140, 152, 154–155, 158; on the threat of communism, 173

Oil, competition for, 20; a determining factor in sovereignty of states, 30; reserves, 33, 80, 123, 133; for foreign exchange, 44; omnipresence in Near East, 58–61; unimportance in Palestine negotiations, 114; Arab League threats to concessions, 153
Open Door, the, 128–131
Ottoman Empire, 25, 29, 35–36

Pachachi, Muzahim al-, 167
Palestine, U.N. problems in, 21; international administration of, 30; British problems in, 30, 34; parti-

tion of, 39; armistice agreements on, 72–73; mandate in, 93, 128; Big Three rivalry in, 94; Stern Gang in, 98; General Nuri on, 139, 140; Arab Congress declares Abdullah king of, 169
Pan-Arabism, 137–138, 139, 141
Paris, peace conference (1949), 68; meeting on Palestine (1948), 116
Parthia, 28
Persia, rise of, 27
Persian Gulf, oil reserves, 59, 122–123
Piedmont, Arab desire to possess, 137–138
Point Four Program, 22, 39, 52–53, 173
Poland, 25
Polybius, theories of, 24
Pompey, Near East rule by, 28
Population, increase of, 61–62
Porte, the, 127
Portugal, 25
Poverty, impelling reality of, 43–44
Prussia, alliance with Great Britain, 25
Ptolemies, rule in Egypt, 28

Qatar, oil reserves in, 59
Quwatli, Shukri al-, President of Syria, 150; corruption in regime, 156; opposition to, 160

Raschid Ali, Pan-Arabism of, 138; repudiation by Abdullah of, 141
Red Line Agreement, 120, 127
Refugee problem, Arabian, 73, 99–100, 117–118; absolute priority of, 101; Jewish, 153
Reza Shah Pahlavi, 119–120
Rhodes, armistice negotiations at, 70–71, 117
Rice, staple of Liberia, 53
Riley, Brig.-Gen. William E., 99
Rome, rule under Pompey, 28
Roosevelt, Franklin D., pledge to Ibn Sa'ud, 153
Royal-Dutch Shell group, 126
Rural labor, in Egypt, 188–189